SILVER CLAY
with style

22 unique & stylish silver clay
jewellery projects to make,
wear & enjoy!

NATALIA COLMAN

All photography by David Airey unless otherwise noted.

Colman, Natalia
Silver Clay with Style : 22 beautiful silver clay jewellery projects to make, wear & enjoy!

Editor: Sally Stevens
Interior design and typesetting: Pantek Media, Maidstone, Kent
Produced by: Natalia Colman

Printed and bound in the UK by the MPG Books Group, Bodmin and King's Lynn

First printing: 2011

ISBN: 978-0-9570968-0-6

This book is dedicated to my beautiful daughter Estella whose love and enthusiasm has helped me every step of the way. Thank you for critiquing my projects, for always helping me, for being the perfect jewellery-making companion and always lifting my spirits.

CONTENTS

★ ★ ★ ★ ★ ★ ★ ★ ★ ★ ★ ★ ★ ★ ★

Section 2 – Pendants and Necklaces

Section 3 – Bracelets, bangles and cuffs

Section 4 – Rings, brooches and earrings

Section 5 – Men's jewellery

ACKNOWLEDGEMENTS

★ ★

Ever since I was a little girl I've imagined writing my own book so producing this has been a dream come true. It combines the two things I love most, writing and making jewellery, a match made in heaven.

I'm lucky to come from long line of creative women. My mother, Rosalba, is talented at so many different crafts. She influenced me hugely in my creativity and continues to do so with her wonderful ideas. My grandmother was excellent at crochet and embroidery, and my great grandmother Natalia, my namesake, was a big inspiration to me when I was growing up. She was an amazing cook, could turn her hand to any craft and would spend all day, every day making things. My mother and Great Grandmother Natalia taught me the patience to sit and create and showed me the beauty of doing this and the happiness it brings to you and everyone you make things for. They set me on the path to creativity, one that I love and that brings me true satisfaction. Thank you to my father, John, who is a fabulous poet and lyric writer. He passed on his love of writing to me and I am very grateful for this.

To my delight, my wonderful daughter Estella seems to be following in my footsteps. She has been so helpful and encouraging throughout this whole project. She has almost been like my artistic director with her keen eye and useful suggestions, even though she is only 11 years old.

Every project needs a strong team to make it a success. I would never have been able to bring this book to you if it wasn't for the very talented David Airey. He worked his magic with the camera and captured each step of the journey and also the beauty of the jewellery. Thank you David for always believing in me and supporting me in making this dream a reality. You have helped me more than you will ever know. I would like to thank Sally Stevens for her excellent work editing this book and for being such a joy to work with. She appeared in my life just at the right moment and this has rein-forced my faith in serendipity. Sally, you have such a keen eye and are so skillful in finding just the right words.

I want to say a huge thank you to Steve Bennett and Paula Bennett of Jewellery Maker TV, for putting their faith in me and including me in their team of Guest Designers. It's a privilege to be able to make designs with their beautiful beads and run their metal clay workshops.

I've been inspired along the way in developing my silver clay skills by many of the talented artists, teachers and designers who have been so generous in sharing their skills and knowledge. A special thank you to Melanie Blaikie whose excellent masterclass started me off on my love affair with silver clay. Thank you also to Lisa Pavelka and Hattie Sanderson whose work, spirit and energy I admire greatly. You are so generous in passing on your ideas and advice to others and are a credit to the metal clay community.

I have run many workshops over the years and this is an aspect of my work that I enjoy so much. Thank you to every single one of the wonderful ladies and gentlemen who have come along to learn with me. You have all taught me more than you will ever know. We have had so much fun in these workshops and I feel very proud that you chose me to be your teacher.

My biggest thank you goes to you for buying this book. I've enjoyed every minute of designing each piece and at times couldn't contain my excitement as I started to bring each of my new designs to life. I hope you enjoy choosing the pieces you wish to recreate and have great pleasure and fulfillment in making them and adding your own touch of flair.

Best wishes,

Natalia

FOREWORD

★ ★ ★ ★ ★ ★ ★ ★ ★ ★ ★ ★ ★ ★ ★

by
Steve Bennett

Steve is a gemstone expert, author and Chief Executive of Coloured Rocks Ltd, one of the largest gemstone suppliers in the world and owner of Gems TV, Rocks TV, Gem Collector and Jewellery Maker TV

When I first came across silver clay I was very keen to introduce it to our range of products on Jewellery Maker TV. When I met Natalia and she showed me her designs and just how versatile silver clay is, I was convinced that our viewers would love this product.

Through our Jewellery Maker TV channel we bring many new ideas and jewellery making methods from around the world to our audience. Natalia's skill and enthusiasm has brought our audience the ability to become silversmiths from the comfort of their own homes, using a small range of tools, they can now create beautiful pieces of silver jewellery.

It is clear to see that Natalia is very passionate about working with silver clay, but she also brings diversity to her creations by adding gemstones, wire and polymer clay to make them truly unique.

The aim of our Jewellery Maker TV channel is to teach our audience how to get the very best from our gemstones and wide range of jewellery making products. Television is a great medium for teaching silver clay but Natalia has created a book that is the perfect companion to her shows and DVDs. You can enjoy browsing through this book, gather lots of ideas and follow the step-by-step instructions, or simply enjoy looking at the beautiful silver jewellery. Natalia has created a book that is ideal for the beginner and offers lots of projects and techniques for anyone who wants to extend their skills and knowledge further.

Best wishes,

Steve Bennett

INTRODUCTION

★ ★ ★ ★ ★ ★ ★ ★ ★ ★ ★ ★ ★ ★ ★ ★ ★ ★ ★

As soon as I came across silver clay I was completely hooked. The thought that I could create my own pieces of pure silver jewellery was just too wonderful an opportunity to pass by. I've since discovered that silver clay is quite magical; it seems to have a Svengali-like effect on everyone I introduce it to and I know that it will bring as much pleasure to you as it has to me.

In writing this book I want to bring you a fresh approach to jewellery making with silver clay. To me, jewellery is there to be worn and shown off and is an essential addition to whatever you are wearing. I want to show you what wonderful possibilities silver clay can add to contemporary jewellery designs. Whether it is just a touch of silver you would like to add to your own designs or you have more ambitious projects in mind, there is something here to suit all tastes and budgets.

I hope the ideas in this book inspire you to make your own beautiful pieces. Whether you are making them to wear for your own pleasure or to sell, I hope that you enjoy experimenting with this incredible material and that you will be very proud of the results.

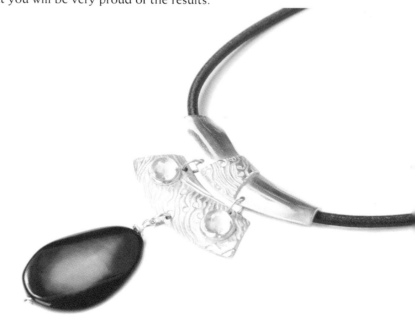

1
SILVER CLAY ESSENTIALS

The question everyone asks me is this: *"Is silver clay really silver?"* The answer is yes. Silver clay is made from tiny particles of pure silver, water and a non-toxic organic binder (bonding agent.) After firing, silver clay becomes 99.9% silver and is known as fine silver; the purest form of silver that exists. Sterling silver has 92.5% silver content because it contains other alloys usually copper to give it strength. The beauty of silver clay is that it has a much brighter appearance and will tarnish less quickly than sterling silver.

In the UK, any pieces that you make with silver clay can be hallmarked and the Assay Office will mark them as 999. Sterling silver has a hallmark of 925.

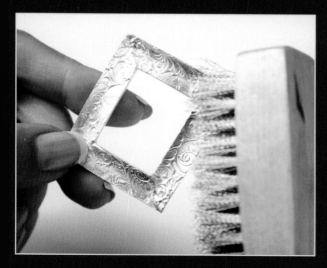

Whilst sterling silver is a stronger metal than silver clay, it is also much more labour intensive to work with. The beauty of silver clay is that you can achieve incredible results in a much shorter space of time, using fewer tools and processes. The reason I love silver clay so much is because of its immense versatility. You can roll it, add texture, create coils and ropes of clay, carve it, engrave it and set stones and fused glass into it. There are so many things you can create with silver clay. From earrings to pendants, rings to brooches, charms to cufflinks. You can use it to embellish glass and ceramics. You can create hollow forms, mould it and even paint it onto living materials such as leaves and twigs. The

★ Silver Clay Products ★

At the time of writing there are two different silver clay products. **Art Clay Silver** is produced by Aida Industries and **PMC (Precious Metal Clay)** is manufactured by Mitsubishi Materials.

The silver contained within silver clay is often reclaimed from computer circuit boards, photographic and x-ray supplies. What I love even more about silver clay is that the processes to produce it are designed to have a minimal effect on the environment.

Mitsubishi was the first to bring their product, PMC, to the market. In 1992 they launched PMC Original. This product shrinks when fired by around 20% to 30% and can only be fired in a kiln. They quickly brought out a more advanced product, PMC+, which can be fired in a kiln or with a gas torch. PMC 3 is their latest product. PMC3 has a shrinkage of 10% to 18% and can be fired using a gas stove, a kiln or a gas torch, so it offers much more flexibility.

Aida Industries followed Mitsubishi into the market with their product: Art Clay Silver 650. This product shrinks by 8% to 12% and can be fired with a kiln, on a gas stove or with a gas torch. It requires a lower firing temperature (a minimum of 650°C hence the name, Art Clay 650) and a shorter firing time than PMC.

Both manufacturers also offer a paste type of silver clay. I have used paste type silver clay in many of the projects in this book, so you will see just how essential it can be. Paste type silver clay is like melted ice cream in its consistency. You can use it to glue clay to clay, fix parts to the clay, and attach two fired pieces together as well as to mend finished pieces. The paste can also be used to transfer patterns and add texture. You can even paint it onto leaves, twigs and flowers to create a perfect replica in fine silver.

You can create your own paste by adding water to the powder created from sanding dry pieces of clay. You may also wish to turn any small left-over pieces of silver clay into paste.

Another product that is an absolute essential for working with silver clay is the syringe type clay. This is silver clay in a pre-loaded syringe. Syringe type silver clay comes packaged in three ways:

★ With colour-coded tips (blue nozzle, green nozzle and grey nozzle) each an increasingly larger diameter

★ A one-tip (green nozzle) package

★ Packaged without any tips

Each of the tips is reusable. The diameter of each syringe nozzle is: Blue Nozzle 0.41mm, Green Nozzle 0.84mm, and Grey Nozzle 1.19mm. The consistency of syringe type is totally different from that of paste type, which is much runnier. Syringe type silver clay is thicker and more controllable. Think of it as though it were like icing for cake decorating. It can be used to add decorative effects such as lines, filigree, faux cloisonné borders, and even hollow balls. It's also excellent as a repair 'glue' to fill cracks and gaps and to attach findings to wet or dry clay pieces, because you can direct it very precisely. I am often asked if it is possible to create your own syringe type clay. My advice is to buy the syringe clay instead of trying to fill an empty syringe yourself. The pre-loaded syringes that come direct from the manufacturers contain a clay that is a specially formulated consistency; it is thick enough to have body but pliable enough to squeeze easily out of the syringe. Creating your own is a hit and miss affair and I've found that it wastes a lot of time and clay in the process.

Art Clay Silver also has two other paste products in its range. These are not essential but you may find them useful as you venture further with your silver clay work. The first is **Art Clay Oil Paste**. This is for use on fired pieces of silver only. It is used to repair cracks or to glue to two pieces of fired clay together. It can be used for both Art Clay Silver and PMC pieces that have already been fired. The second is **Art Clay Overlay Paste** which can be used to add decorative effects to fused glass and glazed porcelain.

For simplicity, all of the projects throughout the book are made using Art Clay Silver 650 (original clay in the navy blue packaging). If you are using a different silver clay product such as **Art Clay Slow Dry** or one of the PMC products, use the same amount of silver clay that is recommended in the materials list at the beginning of each project. Use the same manufacturer's silver clay paste and syringe type clay because Art Clay Silver and PMC products contain different binding agents and should not be mixed before firing. Refer to the firing methods, times and temperatures in Chapter 4 for the silver clay product you are using. Art Clay and PMC products have different firing times and temperatures. For my day to day jewellery work I use both Art Clay Silver and PMC and both are excellent products.

★ Working With Silver Clay ★

Keeping silver clay moist

It's essential that you keep your silver clay in its sealed packaging until the very moment you need to use it, because the clay starts to dry out very quickly.

Always have a small water pump bottle to hand whenever you're working on your projects. This will come in handy to:

★ Add a light mist of water to your silver clay if it begins to dry out whilst you are working with it. Knead it inside a piece of cling film to work the moisture back through the silver clay

★ Keep any spare silver clay hydrated. When you open your silver clay packaging, take the amount of clay you need, then take the spare silver clay and wrap it in cling film. Give the empty packet a light mist of water and place the spare silver clay back inside it then reseal the top of the packet.

★ If you don't intend to use the silver clay again that day, wrap it in cling film and place it inside an airtight container. Also place a piece of damp baby wipe or a wet cloth inside the container to help keep the clay moist longer.

A great piece of advice I picked up from Hattie Sanderson, a world renowned metal clay artist, is to create a mini hydration chamber for your silver clay. Glue a piece of sponge to bottom of a small airtight container. Soak the sponge with water. When you are working with silver clay, place the container upside down over your silver clay; you then can rest assured that your silver clay will stay hydrated until you need it. You also have instant access to your silver clay without having to wrestle with packaging and cling film.

★ Keeping Silver Clay from Sticking ★

Whenever you handle or roll out silver clay, it's essential to have a pot of balm to hand; one that is specially formulated for working with silver clay. Choose a balm such as Badger Balm. This is made from organic extra virgin olive oil, beeswax and castor bean oil. It's a very natural product that won't affect the silver clay and will stop it from sticking to your hands or the surfaces you are working on. Avoid using products such as Vaseline because this contains petroleum which may damage the binding agent in the silver clay.

Alternatively, you can use olive oil to prevent the clay from sticking when rolling and shaping it. Place a piece of sponge into a small dish and add some olive oil to the sponge. Dip your fingers into the sponge and rub a thin layer onto your work surface, texture mats and onto your rolling pin and hands if you are moulding the clay.

Rolling out silver clay

There are many alternative products on the market for rolling out silver clay, such as spacer bars, rollers with attachments and special clay frames; but I always come back to playing cards as a way of rolling an even depth of silver clay. You can simply and easily roll the exact depth of silver clay you need every time, using playing cards. I also use them as a surface to roll my silver clay onto. If the clay sticks to the card I can simply transport it to my warming plate and as the silver clay dries it gently releases itself from the card. Cards can be used as cutting and moulding devices too. You will see examples of this in some of the projects. Playing cards are quite simply perfect for working with silver clay. Another great tip from Hattie Sanderson is to tape cards together and to mark these with the respective number of cards in each pile. Taping prevents the cards from shifting around when you are rolling out your silver clay. Marking them helps you pick up the exact number of cards you need immediately.

When starting out, always roll your silver clay to a thickness of five playing cards. This creates a strong, thick piece of silver when it has been fired. You can roll your silver clay out more thinly, which we will do in several projects later in the book, but be warned, that the thinner the silver clay, the weaker it will be. So you need to take greater care when sanding and finishing your pieces. Fired pieces that are much thinner are also prone to cracking and breaking so do bear this in mind when you are making jewellery that is likely to experience more wear and tear, such as rings and bracelets.

★ Silver Clay Rolling Techniques ★

1   Lay out three rows of playing cards. The first row should contain five cards, the second row should contain one card (you will use this card as your work surface) and the third row should contain five cards.

2   Prop the two outer rows of cards onto the central card. If you don't do this the central card that you will be rolling your silver clay onto raises the height by one playing card, effectively making your clay only four cards thick. Alternatively you could add one more card to the outer piles.

3   Use your fingers to add a very light coating of balm to both your central playing card and your mini roller. Be careful not to be too liberal with the balm, because the silver clay will slide around on your card and you will find it very difficult to roll out. If this happens, lightly wipe the playing card and roller with a piece of paper towel to remove some of the balm.

4   Take your silver clay and use a mini roller to roll it out, using the second playing card in the centre as your work surface. The purpose of using the stacks of cards to the left and right of this is to keep the silver clay that you roll out to an even thickness. You will know when you have reached the exact thickness you require because the cards on the left and right will prevent the roller from making the silver clay any flatter.

★   Shaping and Texturing Techniques   ★

1   You are now ready to create your design. Use cutters, texture sheets or your fingers to mould and shape the silver clay into the design of your choice. Remember, if you want to add a texture to your silver clay, do this before cutting out any shapes from the clay.

2   When adding a texture, place the texture sheet on top of your silver clay. Use your roller to apply the texture. Leave the playing cards in place so that you do not flatten your silver clay too much. Push the roller along the texture sheet from top to bottom in one motion. Apply quite a bit of pressure to ensure that the texture sheet makes a good impression. Do not use the roller to go back and forth because the texture sheet has a tendency to move around and transfers a blurred texture onto the silver clay. Alternatively, you can use your fingers to press the texture into the silver clay. Gently lift the edge of the texture mat to check that you have achieved a good impression. If the texture has not been applied deeply enough, replace the edge of the texture sheet and press down once more using your fingers.

3   Use cutters or a craft knife to cut out your design. Don't worry if your silver clay has stuck to the card you rolled it onto. If you set it aside to dry on top of the card, as the silver clay dries it will release itself from the surface quite quickly. If you do need to lift the silver clay off the surface, use a sharp instrument such as a clay scraper or a tissue blade. I find the edge of a playing card works well too.

★ Drying your Silver Clay ★

If there is any moisture still in the silver when you fire it, the moisture will try to escape to the surface. This can cause the silver to bubble, blister and in extreme cases to explode… **so beware!**

You should allow at least 24 hours for pieces to dry at room temperature. However, you can speed up the drying process up by using a hair dryer, or by placing your piece on a hot plate, inside a food dehydrator, or into an oven or a kiln (around 150°C /320°F).

Below are some recommended drying times and methods for different silver clay products. These are <u>minimum</u> recommended drying times. If you add water to the piece at any time while you are making it, or it is larger than the test piece, you will need to extend the drying time.

The timings given are based on a test piece of 5gms. The hair dryer referred to in the chart is 1200W, held at 3–4 cm away from the piece of silver clay.

Product	Hair Dryer	Hot Plate, Oven, Kiln or Food Dehydrator	Room Temperature
Art Clay Silver 650	15 mins	10 mins at 150°C (320°F)	24 hours
Art Clay Silver 650 Slow Dry	45 mins	20 mins at 150°C (320°F)	24 hours
Art Clay Overlay Paste	10 mins	10 mins at 100°C (212°F)	60 mins
Art Clay Oil Paste	30 mins	30 mins at 100°C (212°F)	24 hours
PMC	1 hour	1 hour at 150°C (320°F)	24 Hours
PMC +	15 – 30 mins	15 – 30 mins at 150°C (320°F)	24 hours
PMC 3	15 – 30 mins	15 – 30 mins at 150°C (320°F)	24 hours

Checking your silver clay is dry

One method of checking if your silver clay is completely dry before firing, is to place the piece on a stainless steel, glass or plastic plate and after 10 – 20 seconds pick up the piece. If there is no cloud of condensation, it is dry.

It is easiest to check for condensation on a mirrored or black surface. A word of caution here; sometimes drying a larger or very thick piece of clay with a hairdryer can dry out the surface but the centre is still moist. In this case the condensation test doesn't work. For pieces like these, ideally you should allow them to dry for 24 hours.

★ Reconstituting Silver Clay ★

There will be occasions when you find that you create a design and that you don't like how it has turned out. You may also find that silver clay you have opened and stored may dry up and go hard. Don't panic, it is possible to reconstitute the silver clay back into its original lump form.

1 Take the piece of hard silver clay and place it in a mortar. Use a pestle to grind the silver clay into a fine powder. You can also use a coffee grinder but be careful to clean it out thoroughly afterwards, or use it specifically for grinding silver clay from now on.

2 Wrap a piece of hosiery tightly over a small container (7 – 10 denier tights work well for this purpose). Place the silver clay powder on top of the hosiery, this acts like a sieve. Use a small brush to push the powder through the holes in the hosiery.

3 Any lumps of silver clay will remain on top and the powder will pass easily through the holes. Return the lumps of clay to the mortar and grind them again more finely. Repeat the process.

4 Remove the hosiery and add some water to the clay powder drop by drop.

5 Use a palette knife to bind the powder and water together to reconstitute it back into a lump clay. If you have added too much water the clay will be sticky. Allow the clay to dry at room temperature. Keep checking it every few minutes to prevent it from drying out. When the silver clay is pliable and feels like normal clay again it is ready to use.

Reconstituted clay does not have the same consistency as silver clay that is fresh from the packet but you are still able to use it in the same way. This reconstituted clay is perfect for using with textured pieces or when casting from a mould.

★ Firing your Silver Clay ★

Firing is the process for turning silver clay into pure silver. This is where the magic happens. No matter which method you use to fire your pieces, the process is the same: burning the organic binders off and sintering the silver particles to increase strength. In the end, you have a piece of 99.9% fine silver, just between 8 – 12% percent smaller and with all the fine detail and shape of the pre-fired piece.

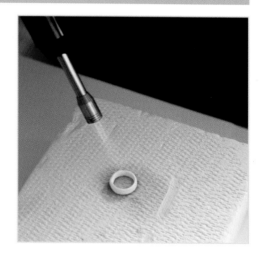

There are three different methods for firing silver clay. You can use a kiln to fire all types of silver clay. For certain types of silver clay you can also use a gas torch and a gas stove.

Gas stovetop firing

If you have a gas stovetop or a portable camping stove, this is a very convenient method of firing silver clay.

The following products can be fired using this method:

★ Art Clay Silver 650

★ Art Clay Silver 650 Slow Dry

★ Art Clay Paste Type

★ Art Clay Syringe Type

★ PMC 3

★ PMC 3 Paste Type

★ PMC 3 Syringe Type

All you need is a piece of stainless steel mesh large enough to cover and balance on the stove burners; a pair of tweezers or metal tongs, protective gloves and a timer. It's also advisable to wear protective goggles.

Firing silver clay with a gas stovetop or camping stove uses a direct flame. This method works best for small and simple pieces. You can fire pure silver findings and small gemstones (5mm or under) with this method. Items that cannot be fired with this method include projects made with large quantities of organic material, and projects that include glass, ceramic or porcelain.

There is a size limitation for this method. You may fire creations that are no larger than 5cm (L) ×3cm (W) ×2cm (H) and which weigh up to 30gms.

Gas stovetop/camping stove firing techniques

1 **Dry your silver clay completely:** Before firing, your piece <u>must be completely dry</u>. See DRYING YOUR SILVER CLAY for further information.

2 **Confirm the hottest part on the stainless steel mesh:** Place the stainless steel mesh on a gas hob or camping stove. Make sure the stainless mesh is placed at the centre of the gas ring. Then turn on and light the gas. Confirm the reddest part on the mesh.

3 **Place the silver clay piece on the mesh:** Turn the burner off and place your silver clay piece on the spot that glowed the brightest. Turn the burner on to LOW and watch for the binder burning away, You may see some smoke and flame as this happens.

4 **Allow the binders to burn away:** When the smoke and flame stops, turn up the burner until the silver clay glows a rosy pink colour (turn off the room lights to see the colour better). Set a timer for **10 minutes**.

5 **Allow the piece to cool before handling:** When you have finished firing your piece you can leave it on the stainless steel mesh to cool down or quench it in some cold water. Be careful to wear protective gloves and use tweezers or metal tongs to handle the fired piece of silver and the mesh because they are extremely hot.

6 **Cool your fired silver by quenching:** To cool off the fired piece quickly, prepare a bowl of cold water. The bowl should ideally be made of stainless steel or metal. If you are using a ceramic or glass bowl, then hold the piece in the water with a pair of tweezers or metal tongs. Use the pair of tweezers or metal tongs to pick up the piece of silver that has just been fired. Plunge it into the cold water for at least 10 seconds. The silver is now cool and ready to handle. Never quench any pieces that contain gemstones or glass. Allow these to cool at room temperature.

Gas torch firing

This method of firing it is the one where you need to be most alert and in control at all times, because you are directing a very hot, live flame. Most gas torches can reach a temperature of 1110°C (2000°F) so it is easy to overheat the silver and melt it. The good news is that this is also the easiest method of firing and more products can be fired using this method, so don't be put off by the idea of working with a live flame. It just requires you to invest a little time to learn how to fire silver clay with a gas torch. The following products can be fired with a gas torch:

★ Art Clay Silver 650

★ Art Clay Silver 650 Slow Dry

★ Art Clay Silver 650 Paste Type

★ Art Clay Silver 650 Syringe Type

★ PMC+

★ PMC 3

This method works best for small and simple pieces. You can fire pure silver findings and small gemstones (5mm or under) with this method. Items that cannot be fired with this method include projects made with large quantities of organic material, and projects that include glass, ceramic or porcelain.

There is a size limitation for this method. You may fire creations that are no larger than 5cm (L) ×3cm (W) ×2cm (H), and weigh up to 25gms.

1 **Dry your silver clay completely:** Before firing, your piece must be completely dry. See DRYING YOUR SILVER CLAY for further information

2 **Place the silver clay on a firing surface:** Place the completely dry piece in the centre of a piece of fibre board or a firing brick. If you have long hair, tie it back and make sure that you have no loose articles of clothing that can come into contact with the flame. Wear a pair of protective goggles.

3 **Ignite the gas torch:** Direct the flame at a 45 degree angle, at a distance of about 5cm (2 in) from the piece. This distance will vary depending on the torch you are using and the size of the piece.

4 **Slowly rotate the flame around the piece to heat evenly:** You will see a little smoke and flame as the binder burns away. A white crystalline surface will appear. When the piece begins to glow peach on the inside, begin to time the firing (turn off the room lights so you can see the colour of the metal). Continue to heat for the recommended length of time. You may have to alter the distance you are holding the torch to maintain the appropriate colour of the metal.

5 **Avoid melting your silver:** If the piece begins to shine and bubble this means it is beginning to melt. If this happens, increase the distance between the torch and the piece immediately, until the glow is just visible and continue firing until completed. You may wish to fire the piece face down to avoid melting the surface texture on the front.

On the next page are some recommended firing times and methods for the different silver clay products. Always check the manufacturer's current recommended firing times and methods before firing your silver clay pieces.

Product	5g	6g – 15g	16g – 25g
Art Clay Silver 650 Art Clay Silver Slow Dry Art Clay Silver 650 Paste Type Art Clay Silver 650 Syringe Type	1.5 – 2mins	2 – 3.5mins	3.5 – 5 mins
PMC + PMC 3	5 – 10 mins	5 – 10 mins	5 – 10 mins

6   **Allow the piece to cool before handling:** When you have finished firing your piece you can leave it on the firing surface to cool down or quench it in some cold water. Wear protective gloves and use tweezers or metal tongs to handle the fired piece of silver and the mesh because they are extremely hot.

7   **Cool your fired silver by quenching:** To cool off the fired piece quickly, prepare a bowl of cold water. The bowl should ideally be made of stainless steel or metal. If you are using a ceramic or glass bowl, then hold the piece in the water with a pair of tweezers or metal tongs. Use the pair of tweezers or tongs to pick up the piece of silver that has just been fired. Plunge it into the cold water for at least 10 seconds. The silver is now cool and ready to handle. Never quench any pieces that contain stones or glass. Allow these to cool at room temperature.

Kiln firing

Kiln firing is the most dependable and accurate method of firing all silver clay types. You can fire bigger pieces of silver clay and there is no restriction on the size of precious stones or cubic zirconia that can be fired using this method. Items that must be fired in a kiln include projects made with large quantities of organic material, and projects that include brass, copper, glass, ceramic or porcelain.

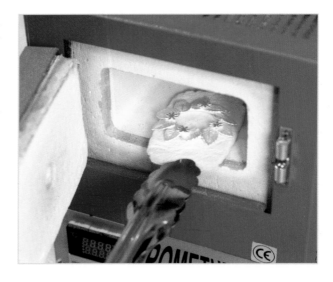

If you kiln fire your silver clay at the hottest temperature for a longer time than stated, these pieces will shrink a little more than they would if you used other firing methods. There is no harm in doing this, in fact the additional shrinkage suggests that the metal is more dense, therefore stronger. If you are kiln firing two identical pieces, such as a pair of earrings, then make sure that you fire them both at the same time.

Use a kiln that is capable of being programmed for the specific temperature and required time to complete the sintering process (holding time). Since there are several kiln manufacturers and models on the market, you'll need to refer to their operating manuals for the appropriate settings depending upon the silver clay project you are making. Each pack of Art Clay Silver and PMC contains instructions about firing temperature guidelines.

Here are some guideline temperatures and timings for the different silver clay products:

Product	650° C (1202° F)	750° C (1382° F)	800° C (1472° F)	850° C (1562° F)	900° C (1652° F)
Art Clay Silver 650 Art Clay Silver Slow Dry Art Clay Silver 650 Paste Type Art Clay Silver 650 Syringe Type	30 mins	10 mins	5 mins	Not recommended	Not recommended
Art Clay Oil Paste	Not recommended	Not recommended	30 mins	10 mins	Not recommended
Art Clay Overlay Paste	30 mins	10 mins	Not recommended	Not recommended	Not recommended
PMC	Not recommended	Not recommended	Not recommended	Not recommended	2 hours +
PMC +	Not recommended	Not recommended	30 mins	20 mins	10 mins
PMC 3	20 mins	10 mins	10 mins	Not recommended	Not recommended

1 **Dry completely:** Before firing, your piece <u>must be completely dry</u>. See DRYING YOUR SILVER CLAY for further information .

2 **Set the kiln to the required temperature:** refer to the manufacturer's operating manual.

3 **Place the silver clay on a kiln shelf:** Place the completely dry piece on a kiln shelf and use metal tongs to place the shelf inside the kiln. You can place your piece inside the kiln when it has reached the required temperature or you can place it in a cold kiln and allow the kiln to warm up. Do not start to time the firing until the kiln has reached the required temperature.

4 **Remove the fired piece from the kiln:** Always wear protective gloves before handling any pieces from inside the hot kiln. Use metal tongs to remove the kiln shelf and place it onto a heat resistant surface. I use a piece of wire mesh placed on top of a fibre brick. You can also place the kiln shelf on top of some wire mesh on your cooker top.

5 **Allow the piece to cool before handling:** When you have finished firing your piece you can leave it on the kiln shelf to cool down or quench it in some cold water. Be careful to wear protective gloves and use tweezers or metal tongs to handle the fired piece of silver and the shelf because they are extremely hot.

6 **Cool your fired silver by quenching:** To cool off the fired piece quickly, prepare a bowl of cold water. The bowl should ideally be made of stainless steel or metal. If you are using a ceramic or glass bowl, then hold the piece in the water with a pair of tweezers or metal tongs. Use the tweezers or tongs to pick up the piece of silver that has just been fired. Plunge it into the cold water for at least 10 seconds. The silver is now cool and ready to handle. Never quench any pieces that contain stones or glass. Allow these to cool at room temperature.

★ Firing Gemstones in Silver Clay ★

No matter how hard a gemstone is or the conditions under which it has developed, only certain gemstones can survive being fired within silver clay.

To avoid disappointment and expense, I strongly advise you to refer to the chart below before you set any gemstones in silver clay. The tests on these gemstones have been carried out by metal clay artisan Judi Weers and Kevin Whitmore of Rio Grande; a supplier of metal clay tools and resources in the USA. These charts are only a guide and results cannot be guaranteed.

If there is a gemstone that you would like to use and it is not on this list, please do carry out your own further research or tests before firing it in silver clay.

Natural gemstones	Survived kiln firing at 650°C (1202°F)	Survived kiln firing at 800°C (1472°F)	Survived kiln firing at 900°C (1652°F)	Survived firing by gas torch
Amethyst	Damaged	Not tested	Not tested	Not tested
Aquamarine	Turned darker	Turned muddy yellow	Turned muddy yellow	Not tested
Apatite	Yes	Turned white	Turned white	Not tested
Aventurine	Damaged	Not tested	Not tested	Not tested
Black onyx	Damaged	Not tested	Not tested	Not tested

Natural gemstones	Survived kiln firing at 650°C (1202°F)	Survived kiln firing at 800°C (1472°F)	Survived kiln firing at 900°C (1652°F)	Survived firing by gas torch
Black spinel	Yes	Yes	Yes	Not tested
Black star sapphire	Yes	Not tested	Not tested	Not tested
Blue sapphire	Yes	Yes	Turned a lighter colour	Yes
Blue topaz	Destroyed	Not tested	Not tested	Not tested
Carnelian	Turned peachy colour	Turned pale	Turned white	Not tested
Citrine	Damaged	Not tested	Not tested	Not tested
Denim lapis	Yes	Not tested	Not tested	Not tested
Green moonstone	Yes	Yes	Turned yellowish colour	Not tested
Green topaz	Yes	Yes	Yes	Not tested
Green tourmaline	Yes	Not tested	Not tested	Not tested
Hematite	Yes	Not tested	Not tested	Not tested
Jadeite	Damaged	Not tested	Not tested	Not tested
Labradorite	Yes	Turned milky colour	Turned milky colour	Damaged
Lapis lazuli	Damaged	Not tested	Not tested	Not tested
Lolite	Yes	Turned a little darker	Turned a metallic colour	Not tested
Malachite	Destroyed	Not tested	Not tested	Not tested
Mexican fire opal	Damaged	Not tested	Not tested	Not tested
Moonstone (Irid white – translucent)	Yes	Yes	Yes	Not tested

Natural gemstones	Survived kiln firing at 650°C (1202°F)	Survived kiln firing at 800°C (1472°F)	Survived kiln firing at 900°C (1652°F)	Survived firing by gas torch
Peach moonstone	Turned a lighter colour	Turned pale	Turned pale	Damaged
Peridot	Yes	Turned a metallic colour	Turned a metallic colour	Yes
Pink tourmaline	Damaged	Not tested	Not tested	Not tested
Oregon sunstone	Yes	Yes	Turned a lighter colour	Not tested
Orissa garnet	Yes	Turned a metallic colour	Turned a metallic colour	Not tested
Rainbow moonstone	Yes	Yes	Turned an irid-blue colour	Not tested
Rainbow topaz	Damaged	Not tested	Not tested	Not tested
Red garnet	Yes	Turned a metallic colour	Turned a metallic colour	Not tested
Rhodolite garnet	Yes	Yes	Turned a metallic colour	Yes
Rose quartz	Destroyed	Not tested	Not tested	Not tested
Ruby	Not tested	Not tested	Not tested	Yes
Smokey quartz	Damaged	Not tested	Not tested	Not tested
Star diopside	Yes	Yes	Yes	Not tested
Tanzanite	Yes	Not tested	Not tested	Yes
Tiger eye	Turned a darker colour	Turned red	Turned dark red	Not tested
Topaz (green & white)	Yes	Yes	Yes	Not tested
Turquoise	Destroyed	Not tested	Not tested	Not tested
White topaz	Yes	Yes	Yes	Not tested

Cubic zirconia are gemstones grown in a laboratory and these survive particularly well when fired within silver clay. Not all colours of cubic zirconia retain their original colour so this list is well worth referring to if you are going to use any cubic zirconia stones within your silver clay jewellery designs.

Cubic Zircona laboratory-grown gemstones	Survived kiln firing at 650°C (1202°F)	Survived kiln firing at 800°C (1472°F)	Survived kiln firing at 900°C (1652°F)	Survived firing by gas torch
Black – opaque	Yes	Yes	Yes	Yes
Champagne – transparent	Yes	Yes	Yes	Yes
Clear – transparent	Yes	Yes	Yes	Yes
Dark aqua – transparent	Turned a purple /blue colour	Turned a purple /blue colour	Turned a purple colour	Not tested
Dark blue – transparent	Yes	Yes	Yes	Yes
Dark red – transparent	Yes	Yes	Yes	Yes
Emerald green – transparent	Turned a brownish red colour	Turned red	Turned red	Not tested
Orange – transparent	Yes	Yes	Yes	Yes
Pale lavender – transparent	Yes	Yes	Yes	Yes
Purple transparent	Yes	Yes	Yes	Yes
Red – transparent	Yes	Yes	Yes	Yes
Tanzanite – transparent	Turned red	Turned dark red	Turned dark red	Not tested
Yellow – transparent	Yes	Yes	Yes	Yes

2
MY FAVOURITE TOOLS & MATERIALS

Having spent a few years working with silver clay I've found that there are certain tools and materials I come back to again and again. They work well for me and are integral to everything I do. I'd like to share these items with you and tell you why they are so indispensible to me.

★ Large Acrylic Roller ★

This roller was intended to be used with polymer clay but I find it is perfect for rolling out silver clay too. It is transparent which is ideal if you need to check that your clay is rolling out smoothly. The weight of this roller makes it easier to roll silver clay especially when the silver clay has come straight out of its packaging.

★ Clay Pick ★

When I first started making jew-ellery with silver clay I only used cutters. It was often frustrating trying to create something that I didn't have a pre-cut shape for. I now make many of my own tem-plates by drawing out a design and cutting a template from card or vinyl. When you place your template on a piece of flat clay you can use the clay pick to cut out the shape very cleanly. The pick has a very sharp needle-like

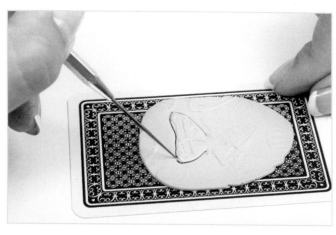

point that goes through the clay like a hot knife through butter. Be careful to store it in its original packaging or push a piece of cork onto the sharp end to keep it clean and to avoid any accidents.

★ Textures ★

Sometimes a design looks so much better with some texture. I collect textures wherever I can find them. There are some really interesting designs available in rubber stamps, texture mats and brass plates. Search craft shops and card making suppliers for ideas. You can also make your own unique textures. This is great fun and also adds true indi-viduality to your designs. Use moulding putty or polymer clay

to take a mould of textures that you see around your home or while you are out and about. A piece of grainy leather can produce a fantastic effect on silver clay, as can textured wallpaper, mesh, net and embossing onto watercolour paper. Why not try texturing your clay by using some string or the bark of a tree to see the effects you can achieve. Let your imagination run wild and create something really different that will have everyone guessing about how you did it.

★ Pin Vice ★

I like to drill holes in my pieces before I fire them. The pin vice has a variety of different sized drill bits that enable you to drill a perfect hole by hand in the exact size you need. If you are drilling near a corner or on a thinner piece of clay the best way to avoid breakages is to start with a very fine drill bit and then to increase the size of the drill, making the hole bigger little by little.

★ Two-Part Moulding Putty ★

Moulding putty opens up so many opportunities to capture an exact replica of anything you would like to cast in silver. I've taken moulds of buttons, textures, beads and even the strawberry shaped lid of a lip gloss jar. Do be careful if you are selling pieces that you have taken a copy of. Use royalty free moulds where possible or you may need to get permission from the designer whose piece you have taken a mould from before selling any silver items you have cast from it. I often find that Mother Nature is the best source of moulds. I've taken moulds of shells and seed pods. I try to collect shells when I visit a beach on holiday or days out and make little silver replicas for a charm bracelet or earrings, to remind me of my travels.

★ Drinking Straws ★

Collect straws of different thicknesses as they are ideal for using to form bails and cut holes. My favourite use for them is as a support for the silver clay when I want to form it into a three dimensional shape.

★ Baby Wipes ★

You can use the wipes to smooth the surface of the dry silver clay and to rub along edges to refine them. The wipes leave a smooth and silky surface. You also use the wipes for cleaning your work surfaces, roller, textures, cutters and your hands to collect any traces of silver clay. Once you have done this don't throw the wipes away. Store your baby wipes in a large plastic bag and when it is full, you can burn the wipes. Any silver will collect into a ball and you can sell this as scrap or melt it down if you wish. With the price of silver climbing as times goes on, you will be very glad that you took the trouble to do this.

★ Snake Roller ★

This is a piece of flat, transparent Perspex. Use it to roll ropes or snakes of clay to create different shapes. You can also roll beads with the snake roller. It is very versatile and incredibly useful.

★ Water Pen ★

The water pen uses the same principle as a fountain pen, except the barrel is filled with water instead of ink. I use my water pen to smooth away cracks in the clay, to help stick two pieces of clay together and to smooth areas where I have applied syringe clay or paste type clay. The pen is also useful for helping to seal gaps. It can be filled with olive oil and used to apply to textures and cutters to prevent the clay from sticking to them.

★ Small Paint Brush ★

When you are sanding dry clay or drilling a hole, instead of blowing the clay dust away use a small dry brush to do this. It allows you to collect the clay dust later to make paste and also allows you to work more cleanly and precisely.

★ Toothpicks ★

These are essential for making holes, supporting the clay to coax into different shapes, mixing the silver paste and for applying it to a small area. Toothpicks are perfect for helping to put holes into the silver clay for findings. Dip the end of the toothpick into some clay balm, touch the table top (the flat part) of the stone. The stone sticks to the balm on the toothpick, enabling you to set it  so that the cullet (the pointed end) goes straight down into the clay. Never throw your used toothpicks away as they will probably be covered in precious silver. Wait for them to dry and scrape off the dried bits of silver to add to your paste jar, or put the toothpicks into your waste silver bag.

★ Brass or Wire Brush ★

You will need this to remove the white residue that is created during the firing process. I love to brush the pieces after firing as it is so exciting to see the silver appearing for the first time, before my very eyes. Use the brush wet with a little liquid soap to prevent the brush from scratching your silver.

The brush can also be used to create a texture on a piece of dry clay. Scrub the brush across the surface of the clay and this creates a unique and very random texture that has a look of brushed steel when the silver is fired.

★ Polishing Papers ★

These come in a variety of different microns and are excellent for creating a smooth surface on your clay before it is fired. Use them dry before firing and use them wet to polish your fired silver. With a bit of time and patience, they really do bring up the most brilliant shine and I use them most of the time. I have grown to love polishing pieces by hand and these polishing papers really do work like magic. Use them in this order:

1 Moss green

2 Charcoal grey

3 Sky blue

4 Pink

5 Mint

6 Cream

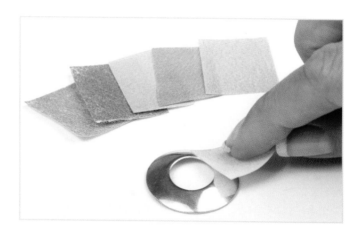

Creating a mirror-like shine using polishing papers

1 Finish making your silver clay piece so that it is completely dry, any imperfections and rough edges have been removed and it is ready to fire.

2 Take a small piece of moss green coloured polishing paper and rub it across the surface of the dry clay in a circular motion, wherever you want the piece to be shiny. Be careful to rub more gently in areas where there is a texture as you do not want to rub this away.

3 Repeat the process working down through the different colours of polish paper. As you reach the mint and cream coloured papers, you will begin to see the particles of silver as the piece will be very smooth.

4 Fire the piece with either a gas stove, torch or kiln and allow to cool.

5 Brush away the white residue from the piece with a wire or brass brush to reveal the silver.

6 Take a piece of sanding sponge and soak it in water. Rub the sanding sponge on the piece of silver in the areas where you would like it to be become shiny.

7 Take a piece of moss green polishing paper and soak it in water. Rub this firmly across the silver piece in a circular motion, in the areas where you would like to achieve a mirror-like shine.

8   Repeat the same process working your way through the different coloured polishing papers. Make sure that you wet the papers when using them on fired silver, so that they polish rather than scratch the silver.

9   Finish by applying some silver polish to the piece. Use a soft cloth to remove the polish and to create a high sine.

10   You can repeat the steps 6 through to 9 if you would like to achieve an even glossier effect.

3
SOME THOUGHTS ABOUT DESIGN

★ ★

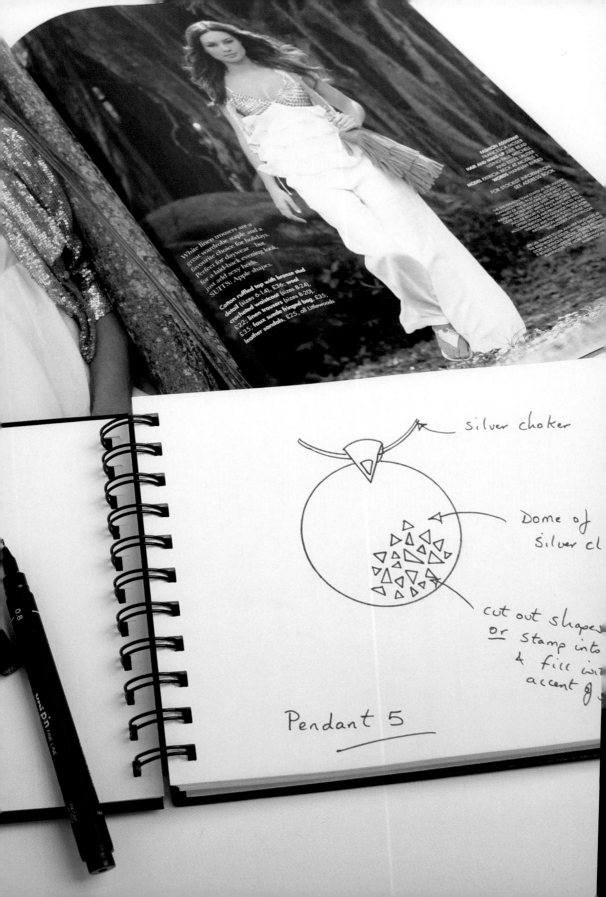

silver choker

Dome of
silver cl

cut out shape
or stamp into
& fill wi
accent g

Pendant 5

Designing your own silver jewellery can be the most rewarding thing in the world. It can also be the biggest headache when you are staring at an unopened pack of silver clay and you haven't the faintest clue what to make with it. Sitting at your work table and willing yourself to turn out something magnificent will not help. The only way to help your creative juices start flowing is to find some inspiration.

I urge you not to open a packet of clay until you have a clear idea in mind. In fact, until you have more confidence in working with silver clay, I'd advise you to map out your projects using polymer clay or Play Dough first, to see how they might look and what the pitfalls might be. This will avoid a lot of disappointment, expense and even tears.

So where will your ideas come from? The best way to create designs and invent new ideas is to look around you. Find yourself a lovely sketch book and start to do little drawings of designs you like as you are out and about. Pay a visit to a museum: The Victoria & Albert Museum in London is a particularly wonderful place to be inspired. Make notes, sketch ideas and let your mind start to assemble these into future designs. I regularly look in fashion magazines and cut out pictures of jewellery I like. I collect all these cuttings in a scrap book and this is a great source of ideas whenever I want to get creative. Go for a walk in the countryside, look at leaves and flowers, observe how cleverly mother nature puts her beautiful designs together: the shapes, the patterns, textures, colours and symmetry, and let this inspire you further.

I also like to critique jewellery designs. I look at jewellery in shops and think to myself: how could this design be improved upon? What would I add to this to make it even more balanced or eye catching?

What you will find happening is that, slowly but surely, ideas will pop into your head when you least expect them to and you'll suddenly be frantic to start making something. This can often happen, very inconveniently, when we have other pressing things to do or even in the middle of the night!

At the jewellery making workshops I teach, my students will often arrive wanting to make a particular piece of jewellery but will be unsure about how to create it. Instead of seeing this as a challenge, I like to approach it with a sense of curiosity. One lady wanted to make a frog from silver clay and had brought along a child's plastic toy frog. We deconstructed its shape and started to draw the frog's component parts. On closer inspection, we discovered that the bulk of the frog was made up of a large body which we observed could be made from an oval ball of clay. It had long thin arms and legs coming off it. These could be thin ropes of clay. The arms and legs had little pads on the end of them and the frog's eyes could be made from balls of clay. We had so much fun as we rolled and cut shapes, sticking them together to create our own whimsical little silver frogs. The  challenge of how to do this project was replaced with artistry and concentration. Both my frog and my student's frog were very different because we had our own unique style, but they were both beautiful and it was clear to see exactly what they were.

Try to approach your designs with care, patience and practicality and you will find that fun and great creativity will come along with it.

Remember that the more you work on creating your designs and practicing your skills, the better you will become. Just remember to enjoy the process.

4
THE PROJECTS

★ Recommended firing times and processes ★

Here are the recommended firing times and processes for each of the projects within this book.

Project	Gas Stove	Gas Torch	Kiln
Beads in Silver Hoods	10 mins	1.5 – 2 mins per piece	650°C 30 mins 750°C 10 mins
Silver Bezel Pendant	10 mins	2 – 3.5 mins (Art Clay) 5 – 10 mins (PMC+ & PMC3)	650°C 30 mins 750°C 10 mins
Lava Bead Necklace	10 mins	2 – 3.5 mins (Art Clay) 5 – 10 mins (PMC+ & PMC3) per bead	650°C 30 mins 750°C 10 mins
Pearl Necklace with Silver Accents	10 mins	1.5 – 2 mins (Art Clay) 5 – 10 mins (PMC+ & PMC3) per piece	650°C 30 mins 750°C 10 mins
Silver Capped Beads	10 mins	1.5 – 2 mins (Art Clay) 5 – 10 mins (PMC+ & PMC3) per piece	650°C 30 mins 750°C 10 mins
Owl Pendant	Not recommended	3.5 – 5 mins (Art Clay) 5 – 1- mins (PMC+ & PMC3)	650°C 30 mins 750°C 10 mins
Natalia's Open Heart Pendant	Not recommended	3.5 – 5 mins (Art Clay) 5 – 10 mins (PMC+ & PMC3)	650°C 30 mins 750°C 10 mins
Silver Trumpet Necklace with Peridot	Not recommended	Not recommended	650°C 30 mins 750°C10 mins
Tribal-Style Necklace	Not recommended	Not recommended	650°C 30 mins 750°C 10 mins
Love Letter Pendant	Not recommended	3.5 – 5 mins (Art Clay) 5 – 10 mins (PMC+ & PMC3)	650°C 30 mins 750°C 10 mins
Art Deco Cuff	Not recommended	Not recommended	650°C 30 mins 750°C 10 mins
Wire Wrapped Bangle with Butterflies	10 mins	1.5 – 2 mins 5 – 10 mins (PMC+ & PMC3) per piece	650°C 30 mins 750°C 10 mins
Silk Cuff with Silver Flowers	10 mins	1.5 – 2 mins 5 – 10 mins (PMC+ & PMC3) per piece	650°C 30 mins 750°C 10 mins

Project	Gas Stove	Gas Torch	Kiln
Polymer Clay Cuff with Silver Accents	10 mins	1.5 – 2 mins 5 – 10 mins (PMC+ & PMC3) per piece	650°C 30 mins 750°C 10 mins
Starfish Earrings	10 mins	3.5 – 5 mins (Art Clay) 5 – 10 mins (PMC+ & PMC3)	650°C 30 mins 750°C 10 mins
Fox Brooch with a Touch of Gold	10 mins	3.5 – 5 mins (Art Clay) 5 – 10 mins (PMC+ & PMC3)	650°C 30 mins 750°C 10 mins
Medieval Ring with Blue Glass	Not recommended	Not recommended	650°C 30 mins 750°C 10 mins
Round Box Ring with Black Pearl	10 mins	3.5 – 5 mins (Art Clay) 5 – 10 mins (PMC+ & PMC3)	650°C 30 mins 750°C 10 mins
Leather Fob Necklace	10 mins	1.5 – 2 mins 5 – 10 mins (PMC+ & PMC3)	650°C 30 mins 750°C 10 mins
Rune Bead Bracelet	10 mins	3.5 – 5 mins (Art Clay) 5 – 10 mins (PMC+ & PMC3)	650°C 30 mins 750°C 10 mins
Carved Pendant	10 mins	1.5 – 2 mins 5 – 10 mins (PMC+ & PMC3) per piece	650°C 30 mins 750°C 10 mins
Antiqued Cufflinks	10 mins	3.5 – 5 mins (Art Clay) 5 – 10 mins (PMC+ & PMC3) per piece	650°C 30 mins 750°C 10 mins

★ Master tools list ★

There are a variety of tools and materials that you will need to use again and again for the different projects within this book. I have compiled a list here so you can gather these in readiness. You may be surprised to learn that many of the tools and materials I have used for the projects can be found around your home or within your craft boxes. Suppliers of the other more specialist materials or tools can be found in the **RESOURCES** section at the back of this book.

Agate burnisher or burnishing tool

Baby wipes

Bead reamer

Beading wire

Bowl of cold water

Brass or wire brush

Caffeinated instant coffee granules

Card or thin vinyl

Clay balm

Clay pick

Clear nail varnish

Cling film

Cocktail sticks

Craft knife

Drinking straws

Fabric glue

Flat nose pliers

Jewellery glue

Kitchen towels

Lighter or box of matches

Liquid liver of sulphur

Mini rolling pin

Needle file

Pencil

Pin vice

Ping pong ball or small round light bulb

Pins

Playing cards

Polishing papers

Ring mandrel

Round nose pliers

Scissors

Sewing needles

Silver polish

Small and large heat-proof dishes

Snake roller

Soft cloth

Sponge sanding pads

Super Glue

Texture plates and rubber stamps

Toothpick

Tweezers

Two-part silicone moulding putty

Water mister

Water pen

Wire cutters

1
A Touch of
Silver

Sometimes just a touch of silver is all that
is needed to turn a piece of jewellery
from simple into stunning.

You don't always need to use large amounts
of silver clay to create beautiful jewellery.
I wanted to show you some pieces that
use other materials with just an accent
of silver. The silver brings a touch of
class and luxury to each piece.

I hope that this section gives you plenty
of ideas about how you can include
silver clay in your jewellery making
without great expense.

BEADS IN
SILVER HOODS

*W*hile working with some pretty beads one day, I wondered how they would look cradled within a little silver hood. My curiosity paid off and I loved the effect of the beads peeping out from their little silver shells. These silver hooded beads can be turned into a necklace or earrings or both.

To make this project you will need:

Materials

★ 10gms Art Clay Silver

★ Three 10mm beads of your choice

★ Three silver head pins

★ 1.5 metres of beading wire

★ 20 crimps

★ 20 crimp covers

★ Necklace clasp

★ Small circle shaped cutter (2cm diameter)

1 Roll out 10gms of silver clay between two piles of four playing cards so that it is a consistent depth. Cut out three small circles using the cutter.

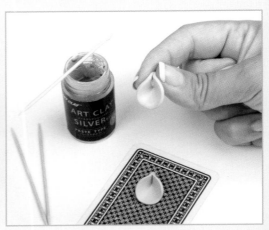

2 Use a cocktail stick to apply some paste type silver clay to the top of each circle. Pinch the sides together and use a water pen to smooth away any excess silver paste. Set these pieces aside to dry.

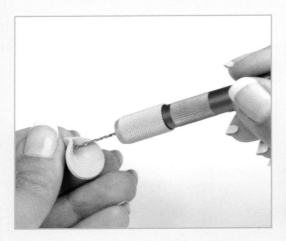

3 Once these pieces have dried out thoroughly, use a pin vice to gently drill a hole up through the centre of the part that has been pinched together. You may need to start off with a very small drill bit and work your way up to a larger drill bit. Be gentle to avoid breaking the silver clay.

4 Use a baby wipe or a sanding sponge to smooth away any rough edges or imperfections. Fire your pieces according to the instructions on page 31. Once the pieces have been fired allow them to cool or quench in cold water. Use a brass or wire brush to remove the white residue and to reveal the silver. Use an agate burnisher to bring a mirror-like shine to the edges of each piece and leave the rest of each piece with a brushed finish.

5 Thread a silver head pin up through the centre of each bead. Push the head pin and bead up through the centre of one of your silver pieces.

6 Use a pair of round nose pliers to create a loop at the end of the head pin. Wrap the excess wire around the base of the loop. Repeat the process with other beads, head pins and silver pieces.

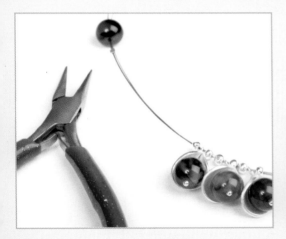

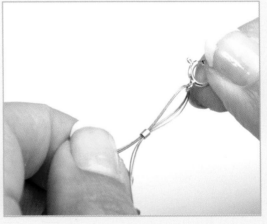

7 Take three strands of beading wire, each one approximately 40cms in length. Thread the wires through the loop at the top of a silver hooded bead. Centre the bead, place a crimp on either side and use the flat nose pliers to press it securely in place. Cover the crimps with a crimp cover and use the flat nose pliers to secure these in place. Repeat the process with the other two silver hooded beads. Thread beads onto the beading wires at various intervals and secure them in place with a crimp at either side to create a floating bead effect. Cover each crimp with a crimp cover.

8 Finish each end of the necklace by threading the ends of the beading wires through a crimp and clasp. Thread the beading wires back through the crimp and secure the crimp in place using flat nose pliers. Cover each crimp with a crimp cover. Your necklace is now complete.

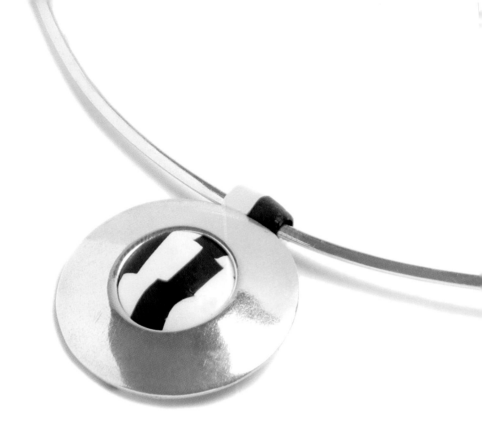

SILVER BEZEL
PENDANT

*7*his silver bezel pendant technique was taught to me by the lovely Christiane Dehaes, a talented metal clay artisan from Belgium. I attended Christiane's fantastic workshop at the World Metal Clay Conference in Chicago in 2011. She showed how she combines silver clay with her polymer clay designs, which opened up a whole new realm of jewellery making to me. You can make the centre of your bezel bigger by using a larger cutter. That way, you can show more of your polymer clay design.

To make this pendant you will need:

Materials

★ 10gms Art Clay Silver

★ Polymer clay in the colours of your choice

★ Ping pong ball or small round light bulb

★ Medium sized circle cutter

★ Small sized circle cutter

1 Roll out 10gms of silver clay between two piles of five playing cards so that it is a consistent depth. Use the medium sized cutter to cut out a circle shape.

2 Remove the excess silver clay. Carefully pick up the circle of silver clay and place it on top of a ping pong ball or small round light bulb.

3 Use the small cutter to cut out a circle from the centre of the silver clay, whilst it is resting on the ping pong ball or light bulb. Remove the circle of silver clay you have just cut out using a clay pick.

4 Set the hollow circle of silver clay aside to dry out. If you are using a light bulb place it inside a small cup or a small container so that it doesn't fall over. If you are using a ping pong ball, place it on top of the medium sized cutter to stop it from rolling.

5 Once the silver clay is completely dry, use a sponge sanding pad and baby wipe to smooth any rough areas or imperfections on the clay before firing. Fire the silver clay according to the processes and instructions on page 31.

6 Once the piece has been fired allow it to cool or quench it in cold water. Use a brass or wire brush to remove the white residue and to reveal the silver. Use some polishing papers to create a high shine on the silver and finish with silver polish. Use an agate burnisher to create a shine along the edges of the piece.

7 Create your own design in polymer clay, following the manufacturer's instructions for conditioning the clay. Use the medium cutter to cut out a circle shape. Push the polymer clay into the back of the bezel and trim away any excess polymer clay with a craft knife.

8 Roll out a 1.5cm long strip of polymer clay, form a loop and press it onto the back of the pendant to creating a handing bail. Bake the polymer clay according to the manufacturer's instructions, whilst it is still inside the silver bezel. Once the piece has been baked, allow it to cool down. Gently remove the polymer clay from the bezel. Carefully place a few drops of Super Glue around the inside of the bezel and stick the polymer clay back in place. Allow the glue to dry for an hour. Your pendant is now complete. Your silver may need another polish to bring back the shine.

LAVA BEAD
NECKLACE

I've used lava stone beads in this design because they are a really interesting material. As the name suggests, they are made from basalt, a type of rock formed during volcanic eruptions. Due to their many holes and bubbles, lava stone beads add great texture, but not a lot of weight, to jewellery designs. Lava stone is naturally rough in texture. Lava stone beads have a smooth coating so they are more comfortable to wear, but still retain all their character.

Lava stone beads are perfect to take a mould from. You can create a perfect replica in silver which makes this necklace a particularly interesting piece of jewellery. It's a real statement piece and certainly a talking point.

To make this necklace you will need:

Materials

★ 7gms Art Clay Silver per bead

★ Two-part silicon moulding putty

★ Four Lava beads

★ 80cm silver chain with large links

★ 1 metre of silver wire 0.6mm or 0.8mm gauge

1 Take two equal amounts of moulding putty from part A and part B and mix them together until the putty is all one colour. Work quickly because the putty starts to cure once it is mixed. Use a large enough quantity of moulding putty to comfortably cover a lava bead.

2 Cover the lava bead completely with the moulding putty and press it firmly onto the bead to capture the shape and texture. Allow to cure according to the manufacturers instructions. You can tell when the putty has cured by pressing the edge of your nail into it. If it leaves an impression the putty is still not fully cured. If it does not leave an impression then your mould is ready.

3 Use a craft knife to cut a line all the way around the mould and release the lava bead from inside. You should have two perfect halves to take a mould from. You can use these moulds again and again and you don't need to add any release agent to the inside of the mould, such as balm or olive oil, because the silicon prevents the silver clay from sticking.

4 Place the silver clay into a piece of cling film and add a light mist of water. Knead the silver clay inside the cling film. Place the moistened clay into both halves of the mould and press down firmly. Ensure that the silver clay covers all sides of the mould: if not, press down into the middle of the mould to create a slight hollow and allow more silver clay to cover the sides of the mould.

5 Set the silver clay aside to dry out in the mould. You can speed up the drying process by placing it in a cool oven or other warm area. Once dry, gently loosen the edges of the mould. The mould is flexible, so you should be able to gently manipulate it to release the lava bead-shaped silver clay. Set the silver clay bead halves aside to dry again until all the moisture is gone.

6 Sand the edges of the silver clay bead halves until they are smooth and form a good fit to one another. Do not sand the face of the bead halves as this might remove the lovely lava bead texture you have created. Use some paste type or syringe type clay to sandwich the bead halves together. Use a water pen to smooth the join and remove any excess silver clay. Set these aside to dry.

7 Use a sanding sponge to smooth around the join of the bead. Fill any holes or seams with more syringe type clay, allow to dry and sand again. Use a pin vice to drill a hole through the centre of the bead for threading. Repeat the process for steps one to seven to make as many beads as you wish. Fire your beads according to the processes and instructions on page 31.

8 Once fired, allow to cool or quench in cold water. Brush away the white residue from firing with a brass or wire brush. If you wish, you can dip the beads in a liver of sulphur solution until they are black. Use some silver polish to remove the black and reveal the silver once more. Your beads are now complete. You can thread them any way you wish to create a beautiful accent for the natural lava beads. They look particularly effective threaded onto a length of silver wire, with a wrapped loop at each end and connected with jump rings to the other lava beads and some large link silver chain.

PEARL NECKLACE
WITH SILVER ACCENT

I love to create these silver teardrop shaped loops using left over clay. Rolling spare clay into ropes makes it go a very long way. You can make lots of these shapes in different sizes, then fire, polish and store them in your findings box to add to future beaded creations.

To make this Necklace you will need:

Materials

★ 3gms Art Clay Silver

★ Syringe type silver clay

★ Two x 35cm strands of 5mm pearl rice beads

★ 2mm or 3mm small clear crystal beads

★ Beading wire

★ Three x head pins

★ Two x crimps

★ Two x crimp covers

★ One x 5mm jump ring

★ Three x 4mm jump rings

★ Necklace clasp

1 Roll the silver clay into a small sausage shape with your fingers. Place the silver clay onto a smooth surface, place the snake roller on top of the silver clay and roll it into a long rope.

2 Stick the two ends of the rope of silver clay together using syringe type clay to form a teardrop shape. Smooth away any excess clay using a water pen. Set the piece aside to dry thoroughly.

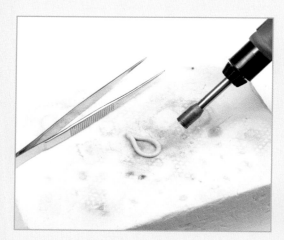

3 Use a sponge sanding pad and baby wipe to smooth the surface of the silver teardrop. Fire the piece according to the process and instructions on page 31.

4 Once fired, allow the piece to cool or quench in cold water. Use a brass or wire brush to remove the white residue and to reveal the silver. You can use an agate burnisher to add a mirror-like shine, or you can leave the piece with a brushed effect if you prefer.

5 Open a jump ring and attach this to the top of the silver teardrop shape, then close the jump ring. Cut two lengths of beading wire; both approximately 40cms in length. Thread both wires through the jump ring at the top of the silver teardrop shape. Centre the teardrop, then thread the pearls and crystals onto both lengths of beading the wire, either side of the silver teardrop shape, in the pattern of your choice.

6 Thread a crystal bead and a pearl onto a head pin. Create a loop at the end of the head pin and wrap the excess wire around the base of the loop. Trim any excess wire and attach a jump ring to the loop. Create three of these pearl charms.

7 Open the jump ring on one of the three pearl charms and attach it onto the silver teardrop, then close the jump ring. Repeat until all three pearls are attached to the silver teardrop. Attach a necklace clasp to each end of the wire and your pearl necklace is complete.

8 You can also create a pair of earrings using the same technique. Simply use smaller amounts of silver clay to create smaller teardrops for your earrings.

SILVER
CAPPED BEADS

I had some left over clay and wanted to use it up in a more exciting way than grinding it back into a paste. I practiced simply squashing the silver clay on top of a bead to create the shape. When the silver has been fired it looks as though the silver has melted onto the bead and is a superb effect. You can do this with any sized bead you like but remember that the silver clay will shrink by 10% when it is fired. So, for example, if you want to embellish an 8mm bead you need to form the shape at the clay stage on a 12mm bead.

To make this project you will need:

Materials

★ 3.5gms Art Clay Silver

★ Two x beads of your choice (8mm)

★ Two x beads of your choice (12mm)

★ Two x pieces of silver wire 6cm in length

★ Two x 4mm jump rings

★ Two x shepherd's hook earring wire findings

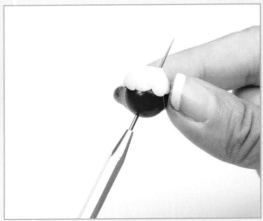

1 Divide 3.5gms of silver clay in half. Roll one piece into a ball and push it over the top of a 12mm bead. Squash the clay down to get an even, thick coverage but make sure that you don't press the clay out too thinly or it will crumble and break when it is dry. Be careful not to cover too much of the bead or you will find the silver clay difficult to remove when it has dried. Repeat the process with the second bead and piece of silver clay.

2 Push a clay pick through the hole at the bottom of each bead to create a hole through the silver clay. Set both of these aside to dry out the clay thoroughly.

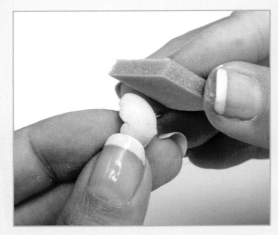

3 Once the pieces have dried, gently remove the silver clay from the top of each bead. Use a sponge sanding pad or baby wipe to smooth away any rough edges or imperfections. Use a pin vice to drill a neater hole in the top of each silver clay bead cap.

4 The bead caps are now ready to be fired. Fire your bead caps according to the processes and instructions on page 31. Once the pieces have been fired, allow them to cool or quench in cold water. Use a brass or wire brush to remove the white residue and reveal the silver. Use polishing papers or an agate burnisher to bring a mirror-like shine to each piece. You can leave the underside of each piece with a brushed finish because this will be hidden by the bead.

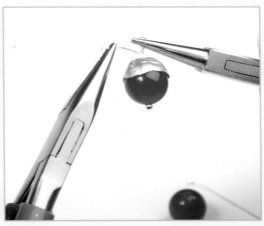

5 Thread a piece of silver wire up through the centre of an 8mm bead. Use the tip of your round nose pliers to turn one end of the wire into a loop, to hold the bead in place.

6 Thread the silver bead cap onto the other end of the wire so that the bead cap sits neatly on top of the bead. Use your round nose pliers to create a loop in the silver wire, then wrap the excess wire around the base of the loop.

7 Open a jump ring and attach the loop at the top of the silver bead cap and a shepherd's hook earring finding to the jump ring. Remember to open and close your jump ring by pushing one end forward and the other in the opposite direction. Reverse the process to close. Repeat the process with the second bead, your earrings are now complete.

8 You can use the same technique on much bigger beads if you wish, which I have done to cap a large drum bead on this necklace. As you can see, the results are stunning.

2
Pendants and
Necklaces

★ ★

*P*endants and necklaces are one of
the earliest forms of jewellery.

The earliest piece of jewellery found was
a copper pendant dating back to around
8700 BC. Pendants and necklaces were worn in
ancient China, India, Rome and Greece. The
Egyptian Pharaohs believed their cartouche
pendants protected them from evil.

If pendants and necklaces are one of your
favourite types of jewellery then you are
amongst good company with our ancient
ancestors. I have included a range of designs
in this section, some accompanied by beautiful
beads and others to be worn as a thing of
beauty in their own right.

I adore owls. To me they are the most beautiful birds. There is a little owl living in the woodland opposite my home and I love to hear his lilting sound in the night.

Owls have long been associated with wisdom, foresight, and are considered by Native American Indians to be the keeper of sacred knowledge. So as well as being a beautiful piece of jewellery, perhaps this owl pendant will bring you extra wisdom too.

To make this pendant you will need:

Materials

- ★ 30gms Art Clay Silver
- ★ Two 4mm cubic zirconia stones
- ★ Large oval shaped cutter
- ★ Small teardrop-shaped cutter (approximately 1 cm wide)
- ★ Medium oval-shaped cutter (approximately 5-6 cm wide)
- ★ Small heart-shaped cutter (approximately 0.8 cm wide)
- ★ Medium heart shaped cutter (approximately 1.5 cm wide)
- ★ Wooden craft stick or small ruler
- ★ Necklace chain or cord of your choice (approximately 46cm)

1 Roll out 20gms of silver clay between two piles of five playing cards so it is a consistent depth. Press a texture plate firmly into the clay but avoid applying too much pressure because this will make the clay too thin. Cut out four large heart shapes and 11 smaller heart shapes. You will need to keep rolling up the clay and re-rolling it to cut out all the shapes. Set all the shapes aside to dry out thoroughly.

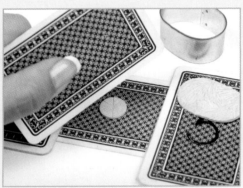

2 Roll out 10gms of silver clay between two piles of five playing cards. Press the texture plate into the clay and then cut out a large oval shape. Roll out the excess clay to four cards thickness and cut two medium sized circles. Press the edge of a playing card into the circles to create the lines in the eyes. Set these pieces aside to dry out thoroughly.

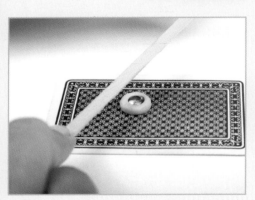

3 Roll two small balls of clay to create bezels for the centre of the eyes. Push a cubic zirconia stone into each ball so that the stone is firmly embedded in the clay. Ensure that the flat top of the stone is level with the top of the clay by pressing down with a wooden craft stick or a ruler. Roll out some spare clay and cut out a small teardrop shape for the beak. Set these pieces aside to dry thoroughly.

4 To create a bail, roll out the spare clay into a long strip, three playing cards thick. Use a playing card to cut along and neaten the edges. Fold the clay around a drinking straw and use syringe type clay to stick the ends together. Cut off any excess clay at the end and leave the piece on the straw to dry out.

5 When all the pieces of clay have dried, sand and smooth them. Assemble the owl by sticking the four large heart shapes to the back of the oval shape. Use plenty of syringe type clay to do this. Gently arrange the pieces until you are happy with their position. Set this stage aside to dry for around three minutes. Build up each layer of hearts in the same way, drying out each layer in between.

6 Once the body is thoroughly dry, stick on the eyes and beak using syringe clay. Roll out two small pieces of clay using your fingers to create the eyebrows and, whilst the clay is still wet, stick these on with syringe type clay. Shape the eyebrows using your fingers and a little water to get the perfect look for your owl. Finally, stick the bail to the back of the owl's head using syringe type clay.

7 Leave the owl to dry out completely. Once dry sand and smooth away any rough edges and imperfections. Fire your owl according to the processes and instructions on page 31. Once fired, allow your owl to cool at room temperature. Use a brass or wire brush to remove the white residue from firing and to reveal the silver.

8 Polish your owl using silver polish and an agate burnisher. Attach a chain or cord of your choice and your owl pendant is complete.

NATALIA'S OPEN
HEART PENDANT

*T*his heart pendant has become my signature piece. I'm a true romantic and I love heart shaped jewellery. In fact, I'm drawn to any heart shapes: I have little hearts hanging from the door handles in my kitchen and a huge beaded heart cushion hanging from the end of my bed. Even the bail on this pendant ended up being heart shaped. So if you like heart shapes too and want to spread a little love, this is the perfect pendant for you.

To make this pendant you will need:

Materials

★ 10gms Art Clay Silver

1 Take 7gms of silver clay (set 3gms aside for the bail). Squash it into a sausage shape. Use the snake roller to roll a long rope of silver clay the length of the snake roller. Hold the snake roller at all four corners and apply equal pressure, rolling it across the silver clay quite quickly. If you find one part of the rope of silver clay is thicker than another, simply apply greater pressure over the thicker area as you roll, to even it out.

2 Use a craft knife to cut the rope of silver clay into two pieces. One piece should be slightly longer than the other. Form the two ropes of silver clay into a heart shape, on top of the snake roller.

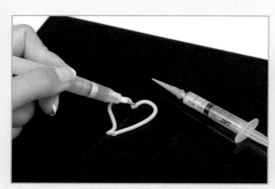

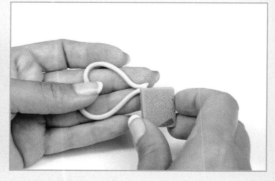

3 Apply some syringe type clay to the top and bottom of the heart, where the silver clay ropes meet, gently press the silver clay together. Add more syringe type clay to ensure that the two pieces are stuck together well. Use a water pen to smooth away any excess silver clay. Squeeze the barrel of the water pen so that the brush part is soaked with water. Run the water pen along the length of the heart to give it a smooth and glossy surface. Set the heart aside to dry.

4 Once the heart shape has dried thoroughly, use a sponge sanding pad to gently sand away any rough areas. Use a baby wipe to smooth the surface of the entire heart on the back and front.

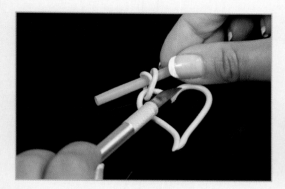

5 Take the 3gms of silver clay and roll a rope of clay approximately 8 - 10cm long, using the snake roller. Wrap the rope of clay twice around the top of the heart shape to create a bail. Use a piece of drinking straw to support the bail.

6 Use a sponge sanding pad to smooth away any imperfections or rough areas on the bail and pendant. The pendant is now ready to be fired. Refer to the instructions on page 31 for firing times and processes. Once the pendant has been fired allow it to cool or quench it in cold water. Use a brass or wire brush to remove the white residue and to reveal the silver.

7 Use polishing papers to bring a mirror-like shine to the piece. Finish by rubbing the piece all over with some silver polish. Remove excess silver polish with a soft cloth or kitchen towel to buff and bring extra sparkle to the silver heart.

8 This pendant looks beautiful when worn with a simple, silver torque necklace. You may also wish to add a length of suede, leather or ribbon and wear it as a longer length necklace. The heart can be made in a larger or small size depending upon your taste and how you would like to wear it.

TRUMPET PENDANT
WITH PERIDOT

*T*he pendant evolved from creating some simple shapes and clustering them together to create a big centre-piece. I love the way that the pattern can be changed and by clustering the silver clay shapes in different ways, you will totally change the design of the pendant. I chose peridot to accompany this pendant, you may wish to experiment with other stones or beads. Peridot is such a beautiful, brilliant green, yet on closer inspection it has tiny, silvery veins running through it, this works extremely well with the silver pendant. As well as being an incredibly beautiful stone, when worn in a necklace peridot is said to be a protector from negative emotions.

To make this pendent you will need:

Materials

★ 20gms Art Clay Silver

★ 40cm strand of peridot stones

★ Sixteen 5mm grey pearls

★ 0.5 metres of beading wire

★ Two crimps

★ Necklace clasp

★ Small circle shaped cutter (1 cm)

★ Medium circle shaped cutter (2 cm)

1 Roll out 20gms of silver clay between two piles of five playing cards so that it is a consistent depth. Cut out three medium-sized circles using the medium cutter. Gather up the excess silver clay, roll it into a ball using cling film and roll out the silver clay again to the thickness of five playing cards. Cut out four small circles using the small cutter.

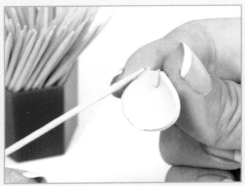

2 Use a toothpick to apply some silver paste to the top edge of one of the circle shapes then pinch the edges together. Repeat this process for all the circle shapes and set them aside to dry thoroughly. Once all the pieces are dry, use a sanding sponge or a baby wipe to sand and smooth away any rough areas or imperfections.

3 Take all the pieces and play around with assembling them into different patterns until you find the pattern you like most. Apply syringe type clay to the back of the three large shapes. Stick these together in your chosen pattern. Use a water pen to smooth away any excess syringe type clay and set aside to dry.

4 Apply syringe type clay to the back of the three smaller pieces and attach these to the pendant in the pattern of your choice. You may need to use quite a bit of syringe type clay for this step. Do not be afraid to apply it liberally because it will help the pendant stay in one, strong piece. Use a water pen to smooth away any excess syringe clay and set the piece aside to dry.

5 Use the left over silver clay and your snake roller to roll a rope of silver clay approximately 3cm long and approximately 3mm thick. Add syringe type clay to each end of the rope and press the rope onto the back of your pendant to create a bail. Apply more syringe type clay if necessary to make sure that the bail stays firmly in place. Use a water pen to smooth away any excess syringe type clay and set the piece aside to dry.

6 Use a sponge sanding pad to remove any rough edges or imperfections at the back of the pendant. Your pendant is now ready to fire. Fire your pendant according to the recommended processes and instructions on page 31. Once the pendant has been fired allow it to cool or quench it in cold water. Use a brass or wire brush to remove the white residue and to reveal the silver. Leave the pendant with a brushed finish, but use an agate burnisher to give a mirror-like shine to the edges of each piece.

7 Take a 0.5 metre length of beading wire and thread your pendant into the middle of it. Thread on peridot beads and grey pearls in the pattern of your choice. I used three peridot beads then one grey pearl. I finished the necklace with two grey pearls at each end.

8 Thread a crimp at each end of the necklace, followed by the necklace clasp. Thread the beading wire back through the crimp and pull the wire tight. Press the crimp in place using flat nose or crimping pliers. Trim off any excess beading wire and your necklace is complete.

TRIBAL-STYLE NECKLACE

*T*ribal-style jewellery never seems to be out of fashion, so a piece like this will be wearable for years to come. This looks like quite a chunky necklace but uses just 25gms of silver clay because it is hollow at the back. The different connecting pieces add to the interest of the design but also give it greater dimension, so it is perfect for those of us who love large scale jewellery. If you prefer daintier jewellery you can still copy the design: simply make it in a smaller scale.

To make this necklace you will need:

Materials

★ 25gms Art Clay Silver

★ Medium sized agate slab (approximately 4cm x 3cm)

★ Two fused glass cabochons

★ Three 7mm sterling silver jump rings

★ 10cm sterling silver wire 0.8 gauge

★ 1 metre of cord or thin leather

★ Silver cord end fastenings

★ Helen Briel texture plate 'Tango'

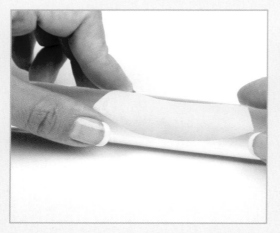 

1 Create some templates for the three different components of the pendant using some card or clear vinyl. You can copy the templates at the back of the book in the Resources section. Roll out 25gms of silver clay between two piles of five playing cards. Roll the silver clay into a long rectangle shape. Place the large template on top of the clay and cut around it using a clay pick or a craft knife. Place the shape of silver clay on top of a curved object such as a rolling pin. Once it has dried and formed a curved shape, remove the silver clay piece from the rolling pin and allow it to dry thoroughly.

2 Roll out the left over silver clay between two piles of five playing cards so that it is a consistent depth. Place the texture plate onto the clay and press down firmly. Lift the edge of the texture plate to check it has made a deep enough impression: if not, press it down onto the clay once more. Gently place the second template on top of the textured clay and cut around it using the clay pick or a craft knife. Place the shape on top of a curved object such as a rolling pin. Once it has dried into this shape, remove the clay from the object and allow it to dry thoroughly.

3 Roll out the remaining clay to three playing cards thickness and press the texture mat firmly onto the clay. Place the smallest template on top of the clay and cut around it using a clay pick or craft knife. Brush some paste type clay onto the back of the piece and stick it onto the middle of the large section of the pendant. Fill any gaps around the two pieces of clay using some paste or syringe clay. Smooth the excess away with a water pen. Set aside to dry. Once the largest component of the pendant is dry, sand and smooth any imperfections with a sanding sponge or baby wipes. Use polishing papers on the face of the piece to make it very smooth.

4 Roll out a thin snake of clay and chop it into three sections. These will form the loops at the back of the pendant to hold the leather or cord in place. Take the largest component of the pendant and pipe some syringe clay onto the back. Press the snakes of clay onto the syringe clay to secure them in place. You may wish to place a thin paint brush or small round object under each snake to help the loops hold their shape. Allow to dry. Then sand and smooth any rough areas.

5 Take the second component of the pendant: sand and smooth any imperfections. Add syringe type clay to the areas where you would like to place your glass cabochons. Press the glass cabochons onto the syringe clay. Extrude some syringe type clay around the circumference of each glass cabochon. Allow this to dry and then add a second application of syringe type clay to make sure the glass cabochons are held securely in place.

6 Use a pin vice to drill two holes at the bottom of the large section of necklace. Use a large enough drill bit to allow 7mm jump rings to pass through it. Drill two holes at the top of the second component of the pendant, ensuring that these line up perfectly with the first part of the pendant. Drill a further hole at the base of the pendant: this is where the agate slab will be suspended from. Fire according to the processes and instructions on page 31.

7 Once fired allow the pieces to cool. Do not water quench the part of the pendant that contains the glass cabochons. Brush away the white residue from firing. Use polishing papers to polish the large component of the necklace to give it a shiny surface. Use an agate burnisher to polish the textured parts of the pendant. Use silver polish to give the pendant components a very high shine.

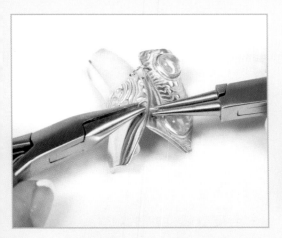

8 Fasten the two components of the pendant together using the silver jump rings. Open each jump ring using pliers, remember to open and close your jump ring by pushing one end forward and the other in the opposite direction.

9 Take a piece of sterling silver wire 10cm in length and thread the agate slab onto it. Make a small loop at the end of the wire using the round nose pliers, to hold the agate slab in place. Bend the wire at the top of the agate slab into a loop at the top and wrap the wire around this loop two or three times. Snip off the excess wire.

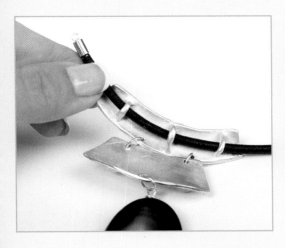

10 Use a silver jump ring to secure the agate bead to the bottom of the pendant. Thread your cord or leather through the loops on the back of the pendant. Cut it to the required length, approximately 45cm and glue some silver cord end fastenings in place onto the ends of the cord or leather. Allow the glue to dry. Once dry, your necklace is complete.

LOVE LETTER
PENDANT

*7*he wonderful love letter texture on this pendant comes from a texture mat created by metal clay and polymer clay artist Lisa Pavelka. At my workshops this is the first texture plate everyone wants to pick up and use, which is no surprise because it looks so effective. I wanted to create a pendant whose shape was determined by the rolling of the clay. I left it exactly as it appeared in front of me without cutting or changing the shape. So when you make your pendant in this way it will be truly unique. I wanted a big, bold pendant but you can make a smaller version if you prefer to use less clay.

To make this necklace you will need:

Materials

★ 25gms Art Clay Silver

★ Lisa Pavelka 'Love Letter' texture plate

★ Silver torque necklace, chain or cord

★ Caffeinated instant coffee granules

★ Boiling water

★ Bowl of cold water

★ Small and large heat proof dishes

1 Roll out 25gms of silver clay between two piles of five playing cards so that it is a consistent depth. Press the texture plate firmly into the silver clay but avoid applying too much pressure because this will make the silver clay too thin.

2 Lift the silver clay off the surface and support the edges using small pieces of drinking straws to create a three dimensional feel to the pendant. Set aside to dry leaving the straws in place until the pendant has dried out thoroughly.

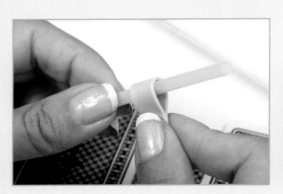

3 Roll out a strip of silver clay (about 3gms) between two piles of four playing cards. Trim the edges to make them straight and then wrap the silver clay around a drinking straw, to create a bail for the pendant. Use syringe type clay to stick the ends of the bail together, then set aside to dry.

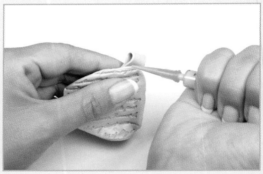

4 Once the pendant has dried, use a sponge sanding pad and baby wipe to smooth the edges and back of the piece. Repeat the process on the bail and use syringe type clay to attach the dry bail to the back of the pendant. Use a water pen to remove any excess syringe clay, then set the pendant aside to dry once more.

5 Once dry, do any final sanding and smoothing then fire your pendant according to the processes and instructions on page 31. Once the pendant has been fired, allow it to cool or quench it in cold water.

6 Use a brass or wire brush to remove the white residue from the firing and to reveal the silver. Use a burnishing tool to burnish the edges of the pedant.

7 Pour some boiling water into a small glass heat-proof dish. Add half a teaspoon of caffeinated instant coffee granules and three or four drops of liquid liver of sulphur. Mix with a pair of tweezers. Pour the hot mixture over the pendant, making sure you do this over a larger bowl or dish so you can collect any spilt liquid. After 30 seconds, rinse the pendant under cold running water.

8 A beautiful, colourful patina will appear on the pendant. If you would prefer a deeper colour, repeat the process in Step Seven. Use silver polish to remove any colour from the edges of the pendant, to create a shiny silver contrast to the centre of the pendant. Thread the pendant onto a silver torque necklace, chain or cord to complete this project.

3
Bracelets, Bangles
and Cuffs

★ ★

*B*racelets, bangles and cuffs are
my favourite types of jewellery.

The first piece of jewellery I ever owned was
a silver charm bracelet and my love of seeing
silver adorning my wrist has continued ever
since. One of the first silver clay projects I
attempted was a cuff. It has been beaten up
and bashed around quite a bit as I take it with
me when I am travelling, but this only seems
to make me like it more. It's a weighty piece of
silver but was worth every penny as it gives me
so much pleasure to wear. I've included this
silver cuff as a project in this section along
with other designs to help you create your own
beautiful bangles, bracelets and cuffs.

Sometimes you may want to make a big silver project, and for me this cuff was a challenge I set myself. I was pleasantly surprised at how well the cuff flexed when I opened it to put it on and take it off. It was inspired by my favourite period ; the Art Deco era of the 1920s and 1930s. This relatively simple design certainly makes a big style statement.

To make this cuff you will need:

Materials

★ 57gms Art Clay Silver

★ Helen Breil texture plate 'Watusi'

★ Small circle shaped cutter (2 cm)

★ Medium circle shaped cutter (4 cm)

★ Large circle shaped cutter (6 cm)

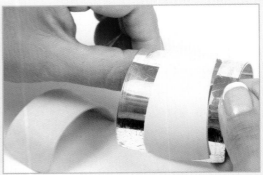

1 Roll out 25gms of silver clay between two piles of four playing cards. Cut out a large circle using the large round cutter. Gather up the excess silver clay, roll it into a ball using some cling film and roll out the silver clay again this time to the thickness of three playing cards. Press a texture plate firmly onto the silver clay. Apply just enough pressure so you get a good impression in the silver clay. Cut out a medium sized circle. Roll out the clay once more to a thickness of three playing cards and cut out a small circle using the small cutter. Set these pieces aside to dry.

2 To create the two sides of the cuff, roll out 25gms of silver clay between two piles of five playing cards. Use a craft knife or tissue blade to cut a strip of clay that is 8cm 3.5 cm. Cut the silver clay so that the shape is slightly tapered, thinner at the top and wider at the bottom. Place the strip of clay to dry on top of a bangle mandrel. Gather any excess silver clay, roll it into a ball in some cling film and add a further 7gms of silver clay. When the first side of the cuff has dried, repeat the process to make the second side of the cuff.

3 When all the pieces of the cuff have dried thoroughly sand and smooth them using a sponge sanding pad and baby wipe to remove any rough edges or imperfections. Brush some silver clay paste onto the back of the medium circle and stick it onto the large circle near the outer edge. Brush more silver clay paste onto the back of the small circle and stick this onto the medium circle near the outer edge. Set these aside to dry out thoroughly.

4 Check for any gaps between the circles. Fill the gaps with syringe type clay and smooth away any excess clay using a water pen.

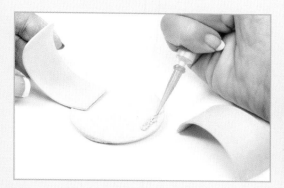

5 Apply syringe type clay to thinnest end of each cuff side of the cuff. Stick both sides to the back of the large circle. Hold the pieces in place for 30 seconds: to enable the syringe clay to dry slightly and make a good join. Use a water pen to smooth away any excess clay. Set the cuff aside to dry out thoroughly, ensure that it is well supported as it is a big piece and it may fall over and break.

6 Check for any gaps between the cuff sides and circle piece. Fill any gaps with syringe type clay and smooth away any excess clay using a water pen. Smooth the entire piece with each colour grade of polishing papers. As this is a large piece of clay with a heavier weight, a kiln is the best method for firing it. Fire it at 650oC for 45 minutes, or at 750oC for 30 minutes. Support the shape of the cuff using some kiln fibre blanket, otherwise the sides of the cuff will fall flat during firing. If this does happen you can gently bend them back into shape when the piece has cooled but is still warm.

7 Once the cuff has been fired allow it to cool or quench it in cold water. Use a brass or wire brush to remove the white residue and reveal the silver. Use polishing papers to create a mirror-like shine on the cuff.

8 You may decide to leave some parts of the cuff with a brushed finish and make other parts shiny. Use wet polishing papers to bring a mirror-like shine to certain areas of the cuff. Finish with silver polish and your cuff is complete.

BUTTERFLY WIRE WRAPPED BANGLE

The design of this bangle was inspired by Jewellery Maker TV's Guest Designer: Laura Binding. Her wire wrapped creations are wonderful and I wanted to make my own version, by adding some little silver butterflies. You can use silver plated wire or sterling silver wire for this project, depending upon your budget.

To make this project you will need:

Materials

★ 10gms Art Clay Silver

★ Embossing folder with butterflies

★ Silver plated bangle frame

★ Four metres of sterling silver or silver plated wire 0.6mm or 0.8mm

★ 2mm Bicone crystals in the colours of your choice

1 Roll out 10gms of silver clay between two piles of four playing cards so that it is a consistent depth. Rub a little clay balm onto the embossing folder, then press it down firmly onto the clay.

2 Use a clay pick to cut out the butterfly shapes. You may need to roll out the clay several times and repeat the process, using the embossing folder to cut out as many butterflies as you would like.

3 Support the buttlerflies to dry as though they are in flight, by bending a playing card at the centre. Once the butterflies have dried use a sponge sanding pad to smooth out any rough areas or imperfections. Your butterflies are now ready to be fired. Fire the butterflies according to the processes and instructions on page 31.

4 After firing, allow the silver butterflies to cool down or quench them in cold water. Use a brass or wire brush to brush away the white residue from firing and reveal the silver. If you wish you can polish the butterflies using wet polishing papers or an agate burnisher.

5 Cut a one metre long piece of silver wire and thread it through one end of the bangle frame. Wrap it around the top of the frame three times to attach the wire securely to the frame. Wrap the wire around the width of the bangle frame. After wrapping four times, wind the wire around the top of the frame twice more. Repeat this process until you reach the other end of the bangle. When you run out of wire: wrap the end of the wire around the top of the bangle. Continue with another one metre long length of wire and repeat the process.

6 Take a small piece of wire approximately 7-10cm in length. Wrap this around the body of a butterfly two or three times and ensure that the ends of the wire are pointing downwards. Position a butterfly where you would like it on the cuff. Weave the ends of the wire through the wire on the bangle to conceal it. Trim any excess wire using wire cutters. Repeat this process until all your butterflies are attached to the cuff.

7 Run your fingers along the inside of the cuff to check that there are no sharp pieces of wire sticking out. Tuck away any sharp ends of wire or trim them with your wire cutters. Thread two bicone crystal beads onto a 3m length of silver wire. Wrap this around the body of a butterfly and tuck the ends of the wire securely through the wire at the back of the bangle. Repeat this process with each butterfly. Your bangle is complete.

*7*he silk cuff actually started life as a cushion cover that I found in a sale. The fabric is beautiful and I had been looking for an opportunity to turn it into a piece of jewellery. The fantastic thing about using fabric and textiles in jewellery is that it can form the bulk of the piece you are making very inexpensively. The silver is still the focal point of this cuff and you can have fun experimenting with different coloured fabrics.

To make this project you will need:

Materials

★ 14gms Art Clay Silver

★ 0.5 metres of the fabric of your choice

★ 0.5 metres of ribbon in the colour of your choice

★ Three 4mm black beads

★ Threads to match with your fabric and ribbon colours

★ Large flower shaped cutter

★ Medium flower shaped cutter

1 Roll out 14gms of silver clay between two piles of four playing cards so that it is a consistent depth. Use a large flower shaped cutter to cut out one flower. Use a medium sized flower shaped cutter to cut out two flowers. Set all the silver clay flowers aside to dry out thoroughly.

2 Once the silver clay flowers have dried, use a sponge sanding pad to smooth out any rough areas or imperfections. Make sure that you sand the face of each piece thoroughly.

3 Use a pin vice to drill a hole at the centre of each silver clay flower. Your silver clay flowers are now ready be fired. Fire your flowers according to the processes and instructions on page 31.

4 After firing, allow the silver flowers to cool down or quench them in cold water. Use a brass or wire brush to brush away the white residue from firing and reveal the silver. If you wish you can also polish the flowers using polishing papers or an agate burnisher.

5 Cut out a strip of fabric measuring 25cm by 16cm. Fold over a 2cm hem on both long edges of the fabric and sew these in place. If you prefer, you can use fabric glue.

6 Fold over a 2cm hem on both short ends of the fabric and sew it in place or secure with fabric glue.

7 Sew the silver flowers to the front of the cuff. Attach a black bead to the centre of each silver flower by knotting your thread and running a stitch up through the hole in each flower. Thread on a bead and go back through the hole in the flower, to the back of the cuff. Stitch back through the bead and fabric several times to make sure each bead is held securely in place.

8 Cut the ribbon in half and sew or glue a length of ribbon to each short end of the cuff. Place the cuff on your wrist and tie the ribbon in a bow. Trim off any excess ribbon. To help prevent the ribbon ends from fraying, carefully use a lighter or a match to gently melt and seal the ends of the ribbon.

*T*his polymer clay cuff is a very classic piece, but the contrast between the black clay and the silver studs adds a little rock chick glamour. I always think that baked polymer clay has a look of smooth leather or rubber. This cuff is made from a pack of polymer clay with simple silver clay accents, making this a cost-effective yet stunning piece of jewellery.

To make this project you will need:

Materials

★ 14gms Art Clay Silver

★ 50gms black polymer clay

★ 0.25 metres of 0.9mm sterling silver wire

★ 0.5 metres of 0.9mm copper or silver plated wire

★ Rubber texture plate

1 Roll out 14gms of silver clay between two piles of five playing cards so that it is a consistent depth. Cut out six small circles and one medium circle. You may need to keep rolling up the silver clay and re-rolling it to cut out all the shapes. If desired apply a texture to the silver clay with a rubber texture plate before cutting out your shapes.

2 Place each cut circle shape on top of a large bead or round object such as a small ball, to form a dome shape. I used the end of a wooden burnishing tool and the ends of my needle files to form the dome shapes for this project. Set all the shapes aside to dry out thoroughly.

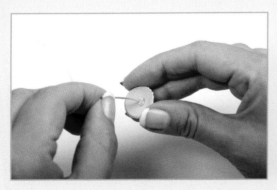

3 Gently remove each dome shape from the object it has been drying on. If the clay is still not completely dry, allow it further time to dry out thoroughly. Once dry, sand and smooth any the edges and surface of each dome. Next, apply syringe type clay to the inside of each dome shape. Use wire cutters to cut seven 3cm lengths of sterling silver wire. Use flat nose pliers to bend the tip of the wire into a right angle. Press each bent piece of wire into the syringe clay inside each dome shape. Bending the end up on the wire will fasten it more securing into the clay when it is dried.

4 Set the domes aside to dry once more. Before firing, sand and smooth any rough edges. Please see firing instructions on page 32 for further information about firing times and temperatures. After firing, allow the silver domes to cool down or quench in cold water. Use a brass brush to brush away the white residue from firing and reveal the silver, then set aside.

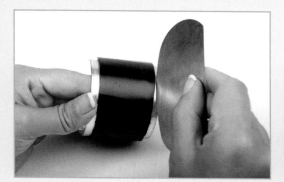

5 Roll out a strip of black polymer clay using either a mini roller or a pasta machine approximately 30 cm in length, 7 cm in width. Place this around a bangle mandrel or use another object such as a tube of thick card to create the cuff shape. Trim off any excess polymer clay along the edges to make it neat. Bake in the oven according the polymer clay manufacturer's instructions. Then allow to cool.

6 Place two pieces of copper or silver plated wire around the polymer clay cuff shape. This will allow the cuff to flex. Leave an excess of wire at the end, this will be trimmed off later. Roll out another strip of black polymer clay of the same length as in step six and place this on top of the wire and baked polymer clay base. Trim off any excess and bake again. Allow to cool.

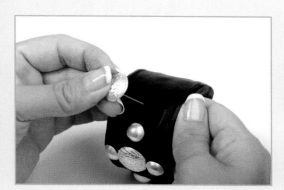

7 Remove the polymer clay cuff from its base and trim off the end of the copper wire so it is flush with the edge of the cuff. Use a clay pick or bead reamer to make holes through the bangle. Push each dome through the hole, wire side down, to secure the domes in place on the cuff. Press the silver wire flat along the underside of the cuff.

8 Roll out another layer of black polymer clay to the same length and width as before and line the underside of the cuff with this to cover up the silver wires. Trim away any excess. Roll a thin length of black polymer clay and place this along the outer edges of the cuff to give it a tidy finish. Bake according to the polymer clay manufacturers instructions. Once cool, your cuff is complete.

4

Rings, Brooches
and Earrings

★ ★

Whenever I teach silver clay jewellery making the most popular request from my students is "can I make a ring?"

Silver clay lends itself beautifully to ring making. There is nothing nicer than making a ring for someone you love. With silver clay you can make the ring a perfect fit and a design that is completely unique.

Earrings are the ideal introduction to making jewellery with silver clay. They are a more cost effective option as tend to be smaller and lighter than other pieces of jewellery. Finally, I wanted to include a brooch as a project in this book. Brooches are making a big comeback as a fashionable and essential jewellery item. Brooches can be so eye catching and add the wow factor to a neutral coat, jacket or waistcoat.

These starfish earrings are another example of how versatile creating your own templates can be. With a starfish design in mind, I drew simple shapes onto card and cut them out to create the templates. I enjoyed the process of adding different textures to the silver clay to make them look as authentic as possible. The stone at the centre is a red garnet and this worked very well with the design. Red cubic zirconia, black spinel, sapphire or Orissa garnet would look equally good. See the chart on page 144 for details of other stones that can be safely fired in silver clay.

To make these earrings you will need:

Materials

★ 14 gms Art Clay Silver

★ Syringe type clay

★ Paste type clay

★ Two 3mm red garnet gemstones

★ Two 4mm jump rings

★ 15cm of sterling silver wire

★ Two shepherd's hook earring wires

★ Six 4mm beads in the colour of your choice

★ Starfish template (see page 144)

1 Create a starfish template by tracing the design on page 144. Roll out 14gms of silver clay between two piles of five playing cards so that it is a consistent depth. Carefully place the starfish template on top of the silver clay and use a clay pick or craft knife to cut around it. Remove the excess clay, roll it into a ball inside some cling film and repeat the process to create a second starfish shape.

2 Use a wire or brass brush and the point of a cocktail stick, very lightly, to create a rough, starfish-like texture on the two pieces of moist silver clay. Set the two starfish shapes aside to dry thoroughly. Once they are completely dry, use a sponge sanding pad and baby wipe to smooth any rough areas or imperfections.

3 Pipe some syringe type clay into the centre of the starfish. Place one of the gemstones onto the syringe clay and press down gently. Pipe more syringe type clay around the outside of the stone to create a silver bezel. Repeat the process on the second starfish. Allow the pieces to dry, then apply a second line of syringe clay around the outside of each stone. Ensure that the girdle of the stone (the widest part near the top) is covered with the syringe type clay. If not, the stone can pop out as the silver clay shrinks during firing. If the girdle is covered well, the silver shrinks and grips the stone tightly in place.

4 Allow the starfish to dry out completely. Next, use syringe type clay to add little dots to create a line of beads on the surface of each starfish. Set both starfish aside to dry out thoroughly.

5 Once the pieces are dry, use a sanding sponge to gently smooth the top of each syringe dot to make it rounded and remove any sharp points that may have been created by the syringe. Use a pin vice to drill a hole at the top of each starfish. The starfish are now ready to be fired. Follow the instructions on page 32 for firing times and processes.

6 Once the starfish have been fired place them on a heat resistant surface, such as a tile or fire brick. Do not quench them in cold water because this may damage the stones. Allow the starfish to cool down at room temperature. This can take around 20-30 minutes. Once the pieces have cooled, use a brass or wire brush to remove the white residue and reveal the silver. Use an agate burnisher to create a high shine on the dots on the surface and the edges of each starfish.

7 Open a jump ring and position this in the hole at the top of one of the starfish. Take a piece of silver wire and cut it to approximately 7cm in length. Thread three beads onto the wire. Use a pair of round-nosed pliers to turn a loop at each end of the wire. Wrap the excess wire around the base of each loop.

8 Attach one loop to the open jump ring and then close the jump ring. Open the loop at the base of an earring wire and attach the other end of the beaded starfish to this. Close the earring wire loop. Repeat this process with the other beaded starfish to complete the project.

ROUND BOX RING WITH BLACK PEARL

*T*his ring incorporates a simple band with an extravagant top. The ring band is one that you can make again and again and when you add different components to the top it creates a totally different design. The top of this ring is the basic method for making a round box. I will also show you how you can add beads or pearls to your ring without having to fire them in place. This opens up a whole new range of possibilities for setting half-drilled beads and stones to your work.

To make this project you will need:

Materials

★ 28gms Art Clay Silver

★ Art Clay ring sizing papers

★ Ring mandrel

★ Black pearl or black pearl-style bead (approximately 10mm)

★ Small circle cutter (approximately 1.5cm)

★ Medium circle cutter (approximately 2.5 cm)

★ 2 cm of 0.8mm sterling silver wire

1 Measure your finger using a ring measuring gauge. You need to allow for the shrinkage of the silver clay, so add 3 ring sizes to the ring size needed. For example, if the ring size you want is 18, you would need to make a ring sized 21 in silver clay, to allow for the shrinkage during drying and firing.

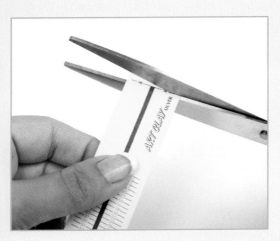

2 Take an Art Clay ring sizing paper. This resembles a Post-it Note with a sticky area on the back. Cut off the excess paper at the cut mark. This is at the sticky end of the paper.

3 Wrap the ring sizing paper around a ring mandrel starting with the non-sticky edge. Adjust the paper until the sticky edge meets the correct measurement line on the paper and stick this edge down firmly.

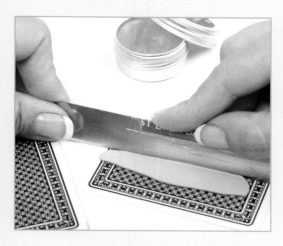

4 Take 7gms of silver clay and roll this into a strip of silver clay to a thickness of five playing cards. Wrap the silver clay strip around the mandrel so the ends overlap. Cut through the overlap with a tissue blade at a slight angle to create a closer joint. Remove the excess clay.

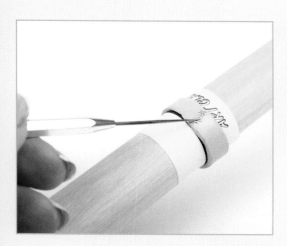

5 Use a clay pick or other sharp instrument to join the two pieces of silver clay together. Make light, dovetail-style incisions to pull the two pieces of clay together. This method creates a much smoother joint on the ring. Leave the ring to dry on the mandrel for 30 minutes.

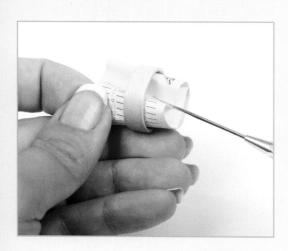

6 Slip the ring off the mandrel by gently wrapping your fingers around the mandrel and twisting the ring sizing paper and not the silver clay band. Carefully insert the clay pick between the ring and the paper and push the paper downwards. Gently crumple the paper inwards to remove it from the silver clay ring.

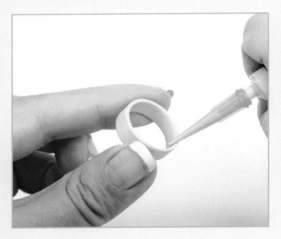

7 Use a sanding sponge to smooth any rough edges. Use some syringe type clay to fill cracks or uneven surfaces. Wet your finger and run it along the syringe type clay to smooth it into the ring join. Allow the ring to dry again. Repeat the process of adding syringe type clay to fill the join and smooth the ring. You may need to do this three or four times to achieve a perfect finish and an invisible join.

8 Roll out 7gms of silver clay into a long strip to a thickness of four playing cards. Trim the edges to make them straight and even, then wrap the silver clay strip around a medium-sized circle cutter so that the ends of the silver clay overlap. Cut through the overlap with a tissue blade at a slight angle to create a closer join. Remove the excess silver clay. Use syringe type clay and a water pen to seal the join. Set the piece aside to dry out thoroughly on the cutter. Take another 7gms of silver clay and repeat this process, this time wrapping the silver clay around the smaller circle cutter.

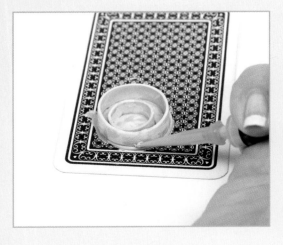

9 When the ring shapes have dried completely, gently remove them from the cutters. Sand and smooth any imperfections. Fill the joins with syringe type clay and smooth with a water pen. Roll out 7gms of silver clay into a circle to a thickness of five playing cards. Use the medium-sized circle cutter to cut out a circle. Press the dried ring shapes into the silver clay circle whilst it is still wet. Set aside to dry. Once dry, use syringe type clay to stick the circle and ring shapes together. Smooth with a water pen.

10 Add some syringe type clay to the centre of the smallest ring shape. Place a small ball of silver clay on top of the syringe clay. Take some sterling silver wire and use some flat-nosed pliers to turn the end up to a 45-degree angle. This helps the silver wire to stay more securely in place. Push the silver wire down through the ball of silver clay and allow to dry thoroughly.

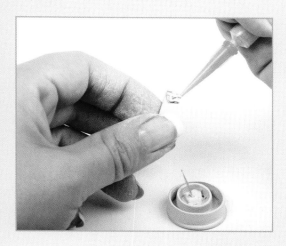

11 Add a generous amount of syringe type clay to the silver clay ring you made earlier. Stick the ring topper to the ring band and hold in place for 30 seconds. Use a water pen to smooth the join between the two pieces and to remove any excess silver clay. Allow to dry and finish with a sanding sponge and dry polishing papers. Fire according to the processes and instructions on page 32. Once fired, allow to cool and use a ring brush to brush away the white residue to reveal the silver.

12 Use wet polishing papers to give a high shine to the ring band, the outside and the top of the ring. Trim the silver wire to a height that allows the pearl or bead to sit flush with the top of the ring. Mix some two-part resin glue according to the manufacturer's instructions. Add the glue to the wire and place the bead on top of it. Hold the bead in place for 30 seconds. Allow the glue to dry for 24 hours and your ring is now complete.

FOX BROOCH WITH
GOLD ACCENTS

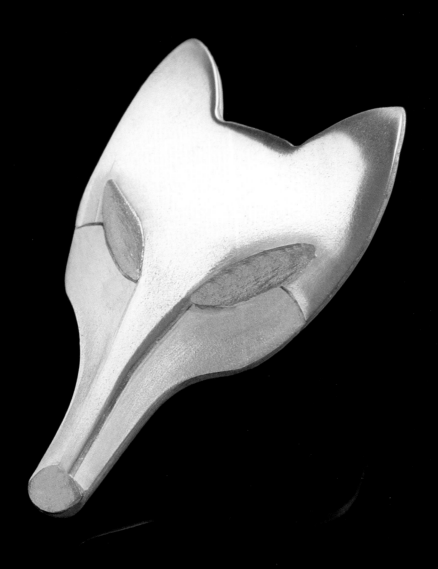

I love to make animal-themed jewellery and this fox is one of my favourite pieces of all. Foxes are symbolic creatures in many different countries and cultures. In Japan they are considered to be one of the rain spirits, and are said to symbolise longevity and give protection from evil. Native Americans consider the fox to be a wise and noble messenger. Foxes generally symbolise quick thinking, adaptability, cleverness and determination which have all been incredibly useful traits for me in writing this book and creating these projects. So perhaps I've received a little help from my beautiful silver fox?

To make this project you will need:

Materials

★ 17gms Art Clay Silver

★ Art Clay syringe type

★ Art Clay paste type

★ Fine silver brooch back

★ Gold coloured gilding wax

★ Fox templates (see page 143)

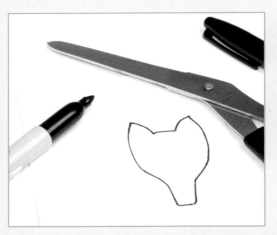

1 Create a template of the three parts of the fox by tracing the design on page 143. You can create your own template using a piece of card or vinyl. If you prefer the fox brooch to be larger or smaller, simply enlarge or reduce the design template using a photocopier.

2 Roll out 10gms of silver clay to a thickness of five playing cards and place the first part of the template on top of the clay. Use a clay pick or craft knife to carefully cut out the template shape. Remove the excess silver clay and wrap this tightly in a piece of cling film to keep it hydrated.

3 Take 7gms of silver clay and add the excess silver clay from the first part of the fox. Roll this out to a thickness of three playing cards and place the second template on top of the silver clay. Use a clay pick or craft knife to carefully cut out the second template shape. Wrap any leftover silver clay in some cling film and set aside.

4 Brush paste type clay onto the back of the second shape. Press it down onto the first fox shape. Use a water pen to smooth away any excess silver paste. Set the piece aside to dry thoroughly. Once it has dried, use a sponge sanding pad and baby wipe to sand and smooth away any rough areas or imperfections. Use syringe type clay to seal any gaps between the two pieces and use a water pen to smooth away any excess syringe clay.

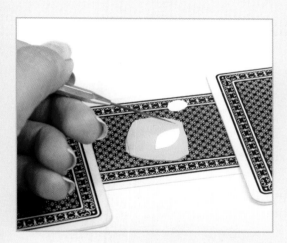

5 Roll out the leftover silver clay to a thickness of three playing cards. Place the eye and nose templates on top of the silver clay and use a clay pick or craft knife to cut out the two eye shapes and a nose shape.

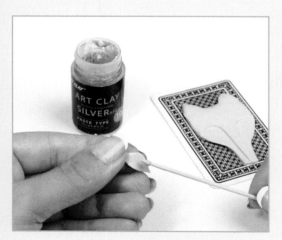

6 Brush silver paste onto the back of each eye shape and stick them onto the fox's face at an angle. Use a water pen to smooth away any excess paste.

7 Set the fox aside to dry completely. When the fox is dry, use a sanding sponge to sand away any rough areas or imperfections. Use some polishing papers to polish the face and the back of the fox, working through the colour grades of the paper.

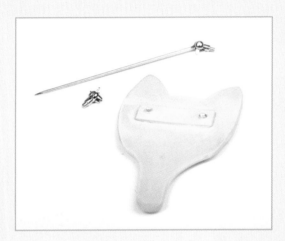

8 Roll out any spare silver clay and cut out a strip of clay approximately 2cm by 2cm. Brush silver paste onto the back of the strip and press it onto the back of the fox. Placed it in the top third of the fox so that the brooch will sit in a balanced position when worn. Unscrew the components of the fine silver brooch finding. Set aside the brooch pin and brooch clasp findings. Sink the other two small brooch findings into the strip of silver clay. Check that both are sitting upright and are aligned. If they are not, then carefully realign them using a cocktail stick and hold them in place for a few seconds.

9 Set the brooch aside to dry. When it is completely dry use a sponge sanding pad to smooth any rough areas or imperfections; then your brooch is ready for firing. Fire according to the processes and instructions on page 32. When the brooch has been fired allow it to cool at room temperature or quench it in cold water. When the brooch has cooled down, brush it with a brass or wire brush to remove the white residue and reveal the silver.

10 Use wet polishing papers to make the top part of the fox's face shiny. Apply some silver polish and buff with a soft cloth or paper towel to bring the fox's face to a high shine. Avoid polishing the eyes and nose.

11 Use a small paint brush to apply gold coloured gilding wax onto the eyes and nose of the fox and allow this to dry for at least 24 hours.

12 Screw the two remaining parts of the brooch into their settings to check that they fit comfortably. Mix a small quantity of resin glue; dip each brooch finding into the glue and screw back in place. Allow the glue to dry. Trim the brooch pin so that it sits inside the clasp and does not protrude. Use a needle file to file the end of the brooch pin to a fine point. Your brooch is now complete.

MEDIEVAL RING WITH
BLUE GLASS

I'm a big fan of using fused glass within my silver clay designs. Fused glass comes in a wide variety of colours and patterns and complements the silver so beautifully. Fused glass is glass that has been layered and fired in a kiln at a range of different temperatures. The glass has previously reached temperatures of up to 900°C (1652°F) so can withstand being kiln-fired within silver clay. It is important to note that silver clay containing fused glass can only be fired in a kiln.

To make this project you will need:

Materials

★ 17gms Art Clay Silver

★ Art Clay ring sizing papers

★ 2cm fused glass cabochon

★ 2.5cm medium circle cutter

1 Measure your finger using a ring measuring gauge. You need to allow for shrinkage of the silver clay, so add three ring sizes to the ring size needed. For example, if the ring size you want is 18, you would need to make a ring sized 21 in silver clay, to allow for shrinkage during drying and firing.

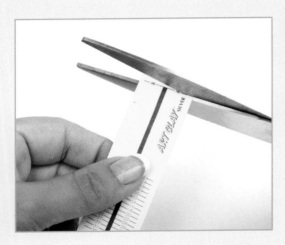

2 Take an Art Clay ring sizing paper. This resembles a Post-it Note with a sticky area on the back. Cut off the excess paper at the cut mark. This is at the sticky end of the paper.

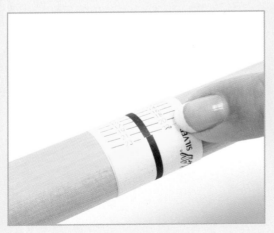

3 Wrap the ring sizing paper around a ring mandrel starting with the non-sticky edge. Adjust the paper until the sticky edge meets the correct measurement line on the paper and stick this edge down firmly.

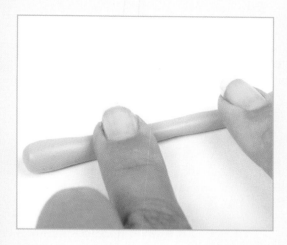

4 Take 10gms of silver clay and roll this into a long rope using your fingers. Roll the rope of clay from the middle so that the ends of the silver clay are more bulbous.

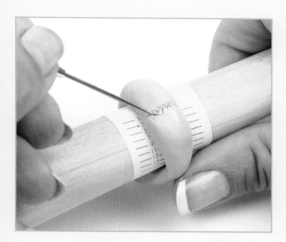

5 Wrap the rope of silver clay around the ring mandrel so that the ends overlap. Cut through the overlap with a tissue blade at a slight angle, to create a closer join. Remove the excess clay. Use a clay pick or other sharp instrument to join the two pieces of silver clay together. Make light, dovetail-style incisions to pull the two pieces of clay together. This method creates a much smoother join on the ring. Leave the ring to dry on the ring mandrel for 30 minutes then gently remove it. Smooth the ring with a sponge sanding pad and use syringe type clay and water pen to smooth any imperfections.

6 Roll out 7gms of silver clay into a circle to a thickness of five playing cards. Use the medium sized circle cutter to cut out a circle. Use a small circle cutter to cut a hole out of the middle. This saves silver clay because the centre of the circle will not be seen as it will be attached to the ring base.

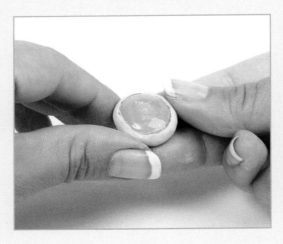

7 Add some syringe clay to the circle of silver clay. Place the glass cabochon in the centre of the silver clay and lift the edges up, pressing them around the cabochon to create a bezel for the glass. Use a damp cotton bud to remove any silver clay that may be on the face of the cabochon. It's important to do this because any unwanted traces of silver clay will fuse themselves to the glass during firing and cannot be removed after firing.

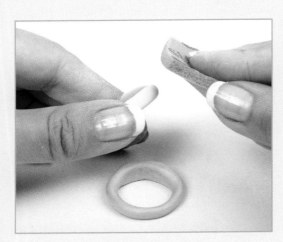

8 Use a sanding sponge to smooth any rough edges and imperfections on the silver clay covering the glass cabochon. Sand and smooth the ring and then use dry polishing papers to smooth each piece.

9 Add plenty of syringe clay to the back of the silver clay piece containing the glass cabochon. Press this onto the ring base and hold in place for 30 seconds. Use a water pen to smooth away any excess silver and to seal any gaps. Set aside to dry thoroughly. Do any final sanding and smoothing before firing.

10 This ring can only be fired in a kiln. Place it in a cold kiln and bring the kiln gently up to 680°C (1256°F). Once the kiln has reached this temperature, fire the ring for 30 minutes. After 30 minutes turn off the kiln, open the door to crash cool the kiln and then leave the door ajar. Do not remove the ring until the temperature in the kiln has dropped to 300°C (572°F). Remove the ring from the kiln and allow it to cool completely at room temperature. Do not quench it in cold water because this may crack the glass cabochon. Once cool, use a ring brush to remove the white residue from firing and reveal the silver. Use wet polishing papers and silver polish to bring the silver to a high shine.

5
Men's
Jewellery

★ ★

*I*t's often difficult to find ideas for men's jewellery designs.

I decided to devote this final section to jewellery specially created for our male friends. Silver is the perfect metal for men's jewellery The designs here range from having quite a modern feel for the more adventurous, to classic designs such as cufflinks. Men's jewellery is challenging, yet great fun to make as it requires us to take a much simpler approach.

*N*ot only is this piece a great size and style for a man, it also acts as a talisman. Each rune has a different meaning so you can create a rune that has significance for the wearer. The rune stone I have used for this design is ingwaz, which represents transformation, inner strength and spiritual growth.

To make this bracelet you will need:

Materials

★ 7gms Art Clay Silver

★ 1 metre of black or dark brown leather cord

★ Rune stone

1 Take an equal quantity of silicone moulding putty from part A and part B and mix them together until the putty is all one colour. Work quickly because the putty starts to cure once it is mixed. Use a large enough quantity of moulding putty to comfortably cover the top and sides of the rune stone.

2 Roll the moulding g putty into a ball and place it onto a flat surface. Push the rune stone, carved side down, into the putty. Push the edges of the putty up around the stone so that it set well into the putty. Leave the putty to cure according to manufacturer's instructions. You can tell if the putty has cured by pressing the edge of your nail into it. If this leaves an impression the putty is still not fully cured. If it does not leave an impression then your mould is ready.

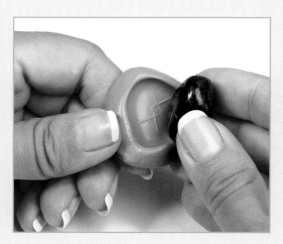

3 Pick up the mould and gently pull the edges apart to remove the rune stone. The mould should be quite flexible but avoid being too heavy handed because it is possible to tear the edges of mould. If you are careful, you can use the same mould again and again. It can also be used for casting polymer clay and resin pieces.

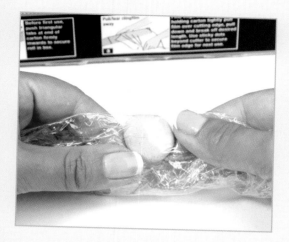

4 Place the 7gms of silver clay into a piece of cling film and give it a very light misting of water. Wrap the silver clay in the cling film and knead thoroughly, working the water through the clay. Keep folding and kneading the clay until it is much softer in consistency. If necessary add a little more water and repeat the process.

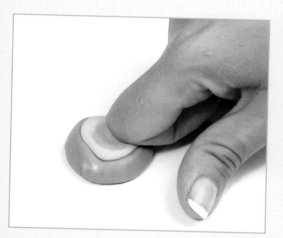

5 If you have used a silicone based moulding putty you do not need to add any balm to the mould first. Push the silver clay into the mould making sure that it is evenly distributed across the mould. Cover your first finger with some cling film and use your knuckle to press the silver clay more deeply into the mould. Leave the silver clay to dry out inside the mould.

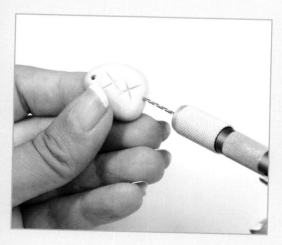

6 Once the silver clay has dried thoroughly, gently pull the edges of the mould apart to release the silver clay from the mould. Use a sanding sponge to smooth away any rough areas or imperfections. Use a pin vice to make a hole at each end of the rune. The hole needs to be big enough for two leather cords to pass through. If the silver clay needs longer to dry out, set it aside until it is completely dry.

7 Fire the silver rune according to the recommended firing times on page 32. Once fired allow the rune to cool down or quench in cold water. Use a brass or wire brush to brush away the white residue from firing and reveal the silver. If you wish you can also polish the rune using polishing papers and silver polish.

8 Take a metre of leather cord and cut it in half. Place the two pieces of cord together and thread them through the two holes in the silver rune. Tie a knot next to each hole.

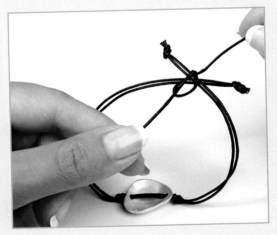

9 You are now ready to create a sliding square knot closure for the bracelet. Cut two more pieces of cord approximately 16cm in length. Tie these pieces of cord around both ends of the bracelet cord.

10 Hold the bracelet cord vertically. Keep the bracelet cord at the centre and the two new pieces of cord on either side of it. Take the piece of cord on the right and pass it underneath the central bracelet cord.

11 Pass the cord on the left over the top of the outer cord and bracelet cord.

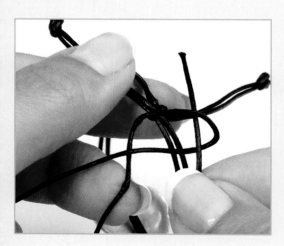

12 Take the left hand cord and thread it through the loop on the right. Pull the two pieces of cord on the left and right tightly together to form the first square knot. Repeat this process starting with the cord on the left tie another knot, then start again with the cord on the right. Continue until you have tied at least six square knots. Trim the ends of the cord. Add a spot of clear nail varnish to make the knot doubly secure.

I've noticed that this style of pendant has become very popular with European young men. I have designed my own version which combines a simple texture on brushed silver with a grained piece of leather. The two textures complement each other beautifully,

To make this pendent you will need:

Materials

★ 7gms Art Clay Silver

★ Helen Breil texture plate 'Tango'

★ 3cm x 6cm rectangle of brown leather (6cm x 3cm)

★ 1 metre of leather cord

★ Silver end clasps for leather cord

★ Riveting tool

★ Brass rivets & eyelets

1 Roll out 7gms of silver between two piles of five playing cards so it is a consistent depth. Press a texture plate firmly onto the clay. Avoid applying too much pressure because this will make the clay too thin.

2 Cut a 2.5cm x 2cm rectangle shape out of the clay using a tissue blade or craft knife. Set this aside to dry.

3 Use a sponge sanding pad or baby wipe to remove any rough edges or imperfections from the pendant. Use a pin vice to drill a hole at the top and bottom of the pendant.

4 Fire the pendant according to the processes and instructions on page 32. Once fired, allow the piece to cool or quench in cold water. Use a brass or wire brush to remove the white residue and reveal the silver. Use an agate burnisher along the edges of the pendant to add a mirror-like shine.

5 Cut a rectangle of leather approximately 6cm x 3cm in size.

6 Position the pendant on the piece of leather, leaving a margin of approximately 2cm at the top of the leather. Use a riveting tool to rivet the pendant to the piece of leather.

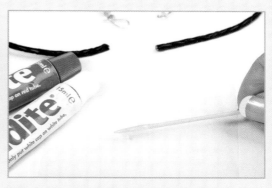

7 Turn the leather over and add epoxy glue along the top edge. Place a drinking straw under the fold so that it remains open, to allow the leather cord to pass through. Leave the glue to dry completely.

8 When the glue is dry, cut a piece of leather cord to fit the neck size you require and thread this through the fold at the back of the leather. Use epoxy glue to secure the end clasps in place and leave to dry. Once the glue has dried your pendant is complete.

CARVED
PENDANT

*D*ry silver clay is an excellent surface to carve into. The random design of this piece is a great way for you to practice carving into the clay. It has a very masculine look and is a perfect talisman for a man. Once you become more confident, you can carve a more detailed and specific design.

You can create whatever shape you like, but I particularly like this small square as I think this is an ideal shape for any man to wear.

To make this pendant you will need:

Materials

★ 7gms Art Clay Silver

★ 1 metre suede cord

★ Small square cutter

★ Bead reamer or ball point pen refill

★ 2mm diameter bead

★ Black oil paint (optional)

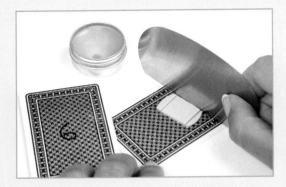

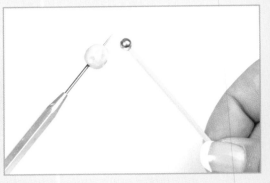

1 Roll out 7gms of silver clay between two piles of five playing cards so that it is a consistent depth. Use the cutter to cut out a square pendant shape from the silver clay. Alternatively you can use a tissue blade to cut the shape you want. Use a narrow drinking straw to cut out a hole at the top of the pendant. Set aside to dry thoroughly.

2 Take a small amount of the excess silver clay (approximately 2gms) and roll it into a ball. Push the ball gently onto a bead reamer or a ball point pen refill. Place a 2nn bead onto the end of a toothpick and press the bead into the silver clay bead to create a dimpled effect. Set the silver clay bead aside to dry.

3 When the pendant has dried, use a sponge sanding pad to sand and smooth the edges. Gently sand the face of the pendant so that the surface is very smooth and has no imperfections.

4 Use a needle file or sharp tool to carve into the face of the pendant. You can draw your design out first using a pencil because any remaining pencil lines will burn away during firing. You may need to carve into the design several times to achieve a good level of depth. It's best to build up the depth of the design gradually rather than using too much pressure too quickly, because this may break the clay.

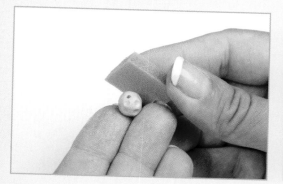

5 When the bead has dried use a sponge sanding pad to sand away any cracks or imperfections. Use a pin vice to drill a bigger hole through the centre of the bead. Ensure that the hole is big enough for the cord to pass through it.

6 Fire your pendant and silver bead according to the processes and instructions on page 32. Once fired, allow the pendant and bead to cool at room temperature or quench them in cold water. Use a brass or wire brush to remove the white residue that builds up during firing. If you would like the bead to be shiny, polish it using an agate burnisher.

7 Polish your pendant further if desired, using polishing papers and silver polish. You may also wish to create an antiqued effect to blacken the carved design. You can do this by dipping the pendant in a liver of sulphur solution and then removing the black colour with silver polish. Alternatively, you can rub black oil paint into the carved design and clean away any excess. If you are using oil paint, leave it to dry for 24 hours.

8 Attach a piece of suede cord to the pendant and secure it with a knot. Cut the suede cord to the desired length and thread one end of the cord through the silver bead, securing with a knot. Create a loop on the other end of the cord and secure this with a knot. Your pendant is now complete.

ANTIQUED CUFFLINKS

*M*any men prefer not to wear jewellery. So if you are looking for something to make for the man in your life, a pair of cufflinks is a thing of beauty that will grace any smart shirt. I used sterling silver cufflink findings for this project. They fired very well and I was able to brush away the fire scale quite easily.

To make this project you will need:

Materials

★ 10gms Art Clay Silver

★ Pair of sterling silver cufflink findings

★ Small square cutter (2cm x 2cm)

★ Helen Breil texture plate 'Tango'

1 Roll out 10gms of silver clay between two piles of three playing cards, so that it is a consistent depth. Press a texture plate firmly onto the silver clay. Avoid applying too much pressure because this will make the silver clay too thin. Cut out two small squares using a square cutter, or a tissue blade or craft knife.

2 Gather up the excess silver clay roll into a ball using cling film. Roll the silver clay out again between two piles of three playing cards. Add a different texture to this silver clay and cut out two slightly bigger squares using a tissue blade or craft knife.

3 Brush paste type clay onto the back of the smaller squares and stick each one to the larger square. Set these aside to dry.

4 Once dry add paste type or syringe type clay to seal any gaps between the two squares and dry once more.

5 Sand and smooth the cufflink squares to remove any rough edges or imperfections. Take care not to sand away the texture from the face of the cufflinks. Roll out two small strips of silver clay and trim it to size (approximately 1.5cm x 0.5cm each). Brush some paste type clay onto the back of it. Turn the cufflinks over and place the length of clay through the back of each cufflink finding. Press down firmly to stick this in place. Use a water pen to smooth any excess paste and to seal any gaps between the two pieces.

6 Allow to dry. Sand and smooth any rough edges or imperfections. Fire the cufflinks according to the processes and instructions on page 32. Once fired, allow the pieces to cool or quench them in cold water. Use a brass or wire brush to remove the white residue and to reveal the silver. Brush the sterling silver cufflink findings to remove the fire scale. Use an agate burnisher along the straight edges of the cufflinks to add a mirror-like shine.

7 Pour some boiling water into a small glass dish, add half a teaspoon of caffeinated instant coffee and three or four drops of liquid liver of sulphur. Mix with a pair of tweezers. Dip the face of each cufflink in the solution and remove it quickly, to check the colour of the patina. Repeat until you have achieved the colour you want, then immediately rinse the cufflinks in cold water.

8 Use silver polish to clean the patina away from the face of the cufflinks. The patina will stay in the texture and the silver will be revealed on the raised areas of the cufflink, showing the beauty and detail of the texture. Clip the second part of each cufflink into place and your project is complete.

TEMPLATES

★ ★ ★ ★ ★ ★ ★ ★ ★ ★ ★ ★ ★ ★ ★ ★

Fox Brooch

Starfish Earrings

Tribal-Style Necklace

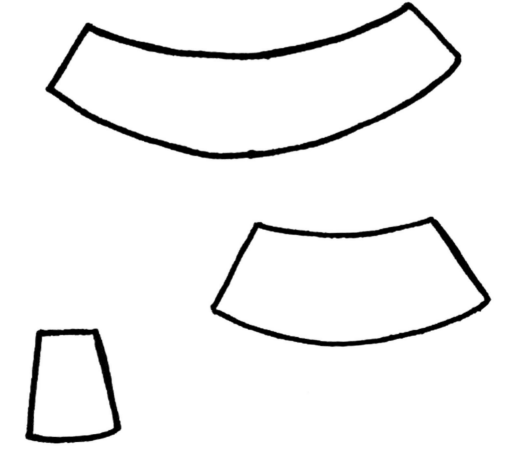

RESOURCES

★ ★ ★ ★ ★ ★ ★ ★ ★ ★ ★ ★ ★ ★ ★ ★ ★

Here is a list of different suppliers I have used to make my projects or who are a stockists of the various materials I have used throughout this book.

Silver Clay Creations

www.silverclaycreations.co.uk

★ Silver clay products, tools & materials, two-part moulding putty, liquid liver of sulphur, ring making materials, workshops, Helen Breil texture plates

Jewellery Maker TV

Eagle Road, Moons Moat
Redditch B98 9HF
Telephone: 0800 6444 655

www.jewellerymaker.com

★ Beads, gemstones, findings , jewellery making accessories, polymer clay, jewellery making DVDs, silver clay kits & products, silver wire, silver & silver plated chain, lava beads, Lisa Pavelka texture plates, cord & chain

Beads Direct

Unit 10, Duke Street
Loughborough LE11 1ED
Telephone: 01509 218028

www.beadsdirect.co.uk

★ Beads, lava beads, gemstones, Swarovski, findings, jewellery making accessories, jewellery making books & magazines, Silver clay products

PJ Beads Ltd

583C Liverpool Road, Ainsdale
Southport PR8 3LU
Telephone: 01704 575461

www.beads.co.uk

★ Bangle frame used in butterfly cuff project, beads, findings

Burhouse Beads
Quarmby Mills, Tanyard Road
Huddersfield HD3 4YP
Telephone: 01484 655675

www.burhouse.com

★ Sterling silver cufflinks used in cufflinks project, beads, findings, jewellery making accessories

Cookson Gold
59-83 Vittoria Street
Birmingham B1 3NZ
Telephone: 0845 100 1122

www.cooksongold.com

★ Silver wire used in butterfly bangle project, jewellery making equipment, fine silver findings

Creative Glass
11–12 Sextant Park, Neptune Close
Rochester, Kent ME2 4LU
Telephone: 01634 735416

www.creativeglassshop.co.uk

★ Fused glass supplies, kilns, gas torches, firing materials, silver clay products, fine silver brooch findings

Palmer Metals
401 Broad Lane
Coventry CV5 7AY
Telephone: 0845 644 9343

www.palmermetals.co.uk

★ Crafted findings riveting tool, rivets & eyelets used in leather fob pendant project

David Airey Photography

david@silverclaycreations.co.uk

★ Jewellery & product photography, jewellery photography master classes

Natalia's two Silver Clay DVDs are also available now at www.silverclaycreations.co.uk

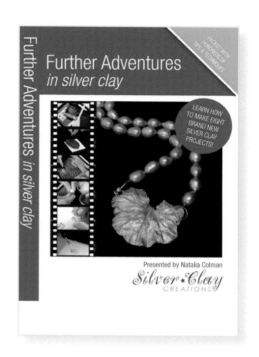

INDEX

★ ★ ★ ★ ★ ★ ★ ★ ★